BALD IS BEAUTIFUL

My Journey to Becoming

⌘ ⌘ ⌘

Jodi Pliszka, M. S.

With Barbara Sharp Milbourn

©2007
Nightengale Press
A Nightengale Media LLC Company

BALD IS BEAUTIFUL

For information about Nightengale Press please
visit our website at www.nightengalepress.com.
Email: publisher@nightengalepress.biz
or send a letter to:
Nightengale Press
10936 N. Port Washington Road. Suite 206
Mequon, WI 53092
Library of Congress Cataloging-in-Publication Data

Pliszka, Jodi,
    Bald Is Beautiful/ Jodi Pliszka
    ISBN:1-933449-10-1
    Mind/Spirit

Copyright Registered: 2007
First Published by Nightengale Press in the USA

May 2007

10 9 8 7 6 5 4 3 2 1

Printed in the USA

What People are saying about
BALD IS BEAUTIFUL

You will always find that there is not shortage of heartfelt stories all over the world today, but it is only a few that stand out, mostly due to an amazing person willing to share their experiences in a way that gives hope and confidence to millions of others. Jodi Pliszka is one of those great people. From the moment I met her, and had the opportunity to be her mentor on American Inventor, I knew that she was driven, committed and has the kind of persona that makes you wish more people possessed. Jodi's story is a journey of hope, love and respect. Her passion for life is something that would sell for millions, if it could be bottled! A truly beautiful person with an amazing heart and a dream that came true. So, here's to Jodi's dream and yours, whatever that may be.

—Peter Jones, British Tycoon, Creator and Judge on ABC TV'S AMERICAN INVENTOR SHOW

I had a chance to meet Jodi while I was hosting the TV show American Inventor on ABC. I was immediately struck by how Jodi stood out like an amazingly bright positive ray of sunshine among the hundreds of inventors who were starving for wealth and fame. I was overwhelmed, inspired and blown away by Jodi's positive energy, inner power and drive to make a difference in the world! It was this unrelenting drive and desire to help others that have empowered her and all those who have had the luck to come in contact with this amazing human being.

This book is a testament to Jodi's desire to reach out and inspire all those in the world who have their own struggles, and to show people that anything is possible as long as you have the courage to believe!

I'm so grateful that I have had the chance to meet Jodi and have her impact my life in such a positive inspirational way. I believe that reading this book will have the same positive inspirational impact!

—Matt Gallant, Celebrated TV Host, Animal Planet's "Planets Funniest Animals," ABC TV's American Inventor, Make A Wish Foundation/Philanthropist

From the moment Jodi walked onto the stage I knew she had a power and presence that could not be dismissed.

Her inspiration and drive can be felt in every page of what I now call "life's instruction manual" that every one should own. Jodi can turn any situation into a winning moment as you will see when you travel on her unbelievable journey. Never say "never" to this powerhouse of energy and positiveness because if you do...be prepared my friends, your life will definitely change.

—Ed Evangelista, Executive Creative Director JWT NY and Judge on ABC-TV's American Inventor.

Jodi Pliszka tells a story of trial and triumph that will encourage even the hardest hearted person to believe reinvention---of your self, your ideas, your dreams--is possible. Bravo to one brave and resilient woman!"

—Mary Lou Quinlan, author "Just Ask a Woman, Cracking the Code of What Women Want And How They Buy" and Judge, ABC's American Inventor

Jodi is a poster child for energy, enthusiasm and never-say die-passion. Read, listen and learn from her if you want a jolt of inspiration to turn your dream into reality.

—Doug Hall, Eureka! Ranch, Founder/CEO, Entrepreneur, Master Inventor, Judge ABC'S American Inventor.

This book is excellent! It brings back memories of my childhood. You have a wonderful way of writing that provides the reader with vivid imagery.

—Senator Mary Lazich, Wisconsin

From start to finish, Jodi's energy inspires you to fulfill your own dreams and create your own victories, savoring every moment of life presented to you! When I put down the book, I instantly jumped into many unfinished projects. Relatable, real, honest, driven, a true breath of hope in challenging times, Jodi sets you on the right path. Every day we are presented with blank pages on which we can write our own story of triumph through perseverance; Jodi shows us how to write through her example!

—Rick Rose, Entrepreneur, TV/Radio Host, contributor to The Word in Season Daily Devotional

Never say never! Read 'Bald is Beautiful' and find the path to success in life; motivation in moving forward exuding positive power and leap into opportunities with incredible inspiration from a real role model mimicking her amazing strength in extraordinary dilemmas. A true treasure!

—Jodie Lynn, Speaker, Internationally Syndicated Family/ Health Columnist and Author, Mom CEO (Chief Everything Officer) Having, Doing and Surviving It All.

I began reading this book one evening and could not put it down. I followed Jodi through each step of her story, feeling her sorrow, her strength and the pure joy of her accomplishments. Her words have inspired me to see that we are all perfect, that we are all beautiful and each of us has the power to bring our dreams into reality. Thank you Jodi!

—Jody Colvard, Founder: FunMoneyGood Network, The Women in Podcasting Directory

Jodi's book is a monument to overcoming - overcoming an abusive relationship, overcoming disease, overcoming a loss of identity, and overcoming self doubt, fear and rejection. Jodi is redefining what it means to be a woman, a human and a spiritual being. I used to see angels as divine beings with long, bright, glowing hair and wings that hovered above those they loved. I now see them as flawed individuals with all of their warts, pimples, bruises and bald heads who dwell among us and embrace those with similar flaws. It is their loving touch that heals. What distinguishes them from other beings are their warm hearts, glowing spirits, firm embrace, and fuzzy insides. Jodi is that angel to me. It's all too true . . .

—Daniel R. Castro, Award Winning Author of Critical Choices that Change Lives. www.dancastro.com

Jodi's life journey truly massages the heart and inspires the soul. While facing insurmountable challenges, she recognizes her own blessings and blesses the lives of others. Jodi's story is a gift of hope to all those in pursuit of discovering their own wholeness. It is the epitome of the joy of being alive.

—Lolly Rose, Founder/Executive Director, Angel On My Shoulder, A registered non-profit cancer support foundation.

The road to recovery, motivation and inspiration begins with Jodi Pliszka's Book BALD IS BEAUTIFUL. This true story on healing and personal success will teach you the power of inner strength and perseverance. Once I started I could not put this book down. It is a great book with a fairy tale ending, that happens to be true. A great read.

—**Dr. Eric Kaplan, Speaker, Best-selling Author,** *Dr. Kaplan's Lifestyle of the Fit and Famous, Dying to be Young*

Jodi is the most amazing women I have ever met. She is brilliant, funny, fun and astonishing. What Jodi has experienced is something that most of us will never know. And to do so with such grace and humility, she is more than a role model - she is what we all strive to be. I fell in love with her during our days on American Inventor and that friendship just keeps growing. A fellow author, speaker and inventor, I have to say I am just continuously blown away with her courage and her ability to be everything she has ever dreamed. This book—which is just an amazing read—is just the tip of the iceberg from what I know you will see from this woman! Jodi is an inspiration to everyone she meets and I am honored to be her friend.

—**Dr. Natalie L. Petouhoff (Dr. Nat The Technocat), Hughes Electronics, Radar Division's "Rocket Scientist," Consumer Product Expert and Invention Coach, ww.drnatthetechnocat.com & www.drnatnews.com**

Jodi Pliszka shares her amazing journey through her life from tragedy to triumph. She touches your soul with her pure honesty and humility. You identify with her incredible life challenges from dealing with depression, self esteem, anger, love, fear, courage and success. Jodi tells her story in a way to help inspire others by giving us the message that we should never give up on ourselves or our dreams. She is living proof that you can overcome the hardest lessons that life can give and turn them into something truly positive and wonderful. From cover to cover you to will be enthralled and empowered with Jodi's optimism of embracing life and what we can learn from the journey".

—**Carol Daly - Owner/Creative Director of Daly Design Group LLC.**

Meeting Jodi was an instant bond for me as a member of "Peter's group" on the show. Reading her book after spending many days with her on the show allowed me to draw on her life experiences and why she wears her passion on her sleeve and is able to transform them to her inspiring pages. The importance of her journey will help you clarify what is really meant by determination. Jodi continues to exemplify throughout the book and her life my own mantra that you need not only intelligence but also an adversity engine to take your goal through to fruition. She had me at "Hello, I'm Jodi Pliszka." I'm sure this vibrant prospect in today's writing establishment will have you too!

—Bobby Amore, American Inventor, Inventor of the Toner Belt

ACKNOWLEDGEMENTS

My very special thanks to my family, Fred and Karen Pliszka, for their love and support. They have parented, grand-parented, business ventured, counseled, healed, encouraged, advised and cheered me more than words on a page could ever recount. To my amazing daughter Jessica, for her bravery during times of separation, her patience and personal assistance while I work at home, her companionship and unconditional love. I'm so proud of you. I love you, and remember, dreams really do come true. To my niece, Morgan, with whom I adore and cherish dearly. To my 'Auntie' Phyllis Bruneau for teaching me that there is a child in us all, and that attitude is everything. To my Grandma Marge, in memorial, for showing me what empathy and caring looks like and for being my guardian angel.

Many thanks to Barbara Sharp Milbourn for helping me write my story. You were an inspiration and joy to work with, an angel in my path.

Thanks to Valerie and Mike Connelly from Nightengale Press for believing in me, for taking care of my publishing and website needs, and for your priceless friendship.

Thanks to the American Inventor TV show, for helping tell my story to your audience and for making my HEADLINE IT! dream come true.

Thanks to the T2 DESIGN team, Paul Berman, Linda Shayne, Dr.Natalie Pethouff, Christina Landers, Brad Sorenson, Matt Pelham and Alicia Hayes for your wonderful prototyping, amazing packaging and product testing. You were delightful to work with and I gladly give you credit for getting HEADLINE IT! where it is today.

Special thanks to my attorney and friend Mark Crossley, Esq. for generously donating his time to my trademark and patent work.

Thank you to my dearest friend Carol Daly, Daly Design, for creating my excellent business cards, brochures and everything HEADLINE IT!. You are a gem.

To my dear friend and PR agent, Scott Lazerson. Thank you for going above and beyond with our excellent PR, for being my business advisor, agent, and go-to man. You are exceptional and a true survivor, the number one PHILANTHROPIST in my book.

Thank you to Martin Berger and Bob Susa at InventHelpSM for sharing in my fairy tale and for the opportunity of spokesperson. I look forward to a long, prosperous relationship.

To my friends on American Inventor; Joe and Jen Safuto (Pureflush), Sharon Clemens (Restroom Survival Kit), Sheryl McDonald (Inbrella), Bobby Amore (Toner Belt), Pat and Vickie Rock (Take a Seat), Mark Major (The Flosser), Joan Colvin (character bear), Erik Thompson (the CATCH), Darla Davenport (Niya Doll), Fransico Patino (the traction bike), Janush Lieberkowski (Spherical baby seat), Jerry Wesley (EZ X GYM) Mark Martinez (SackMaster), and Erin Flinn and Zack Green, show producers. Thank you for an inspiring and memorable two months together. I wish you ALL great success.

Thank you to talented, Ed Evangelista for making HEADLINE IT! a success.. I am honored to work with you. Thanks to my mentor, Peter Jones, for his insight and for being a true gentleman. Thanks to Doug Hall for challenging me, and to another angel, MaryLou Quinnlan for being positive and for her direction on the show. Thanks to Matt Gallant for making me smile and for the hugs after every round. Thanks to the producers, PA's, camera and sound people, directors at ABC and FREMANTLE for giving me the opportunity of a lifetime.

A very special thank you to Dan Castro for being our HEADLINE IT! attorney and my special friend. For his award-winning book, *Critical Choices that Change Lives,* that accompanied me to California and helped me through my struggles. Thanks for letting me be your "bald angel."

Thank you to Rick Rose, Lolly Rose and Mary Long, for always believing in me and helping me on my journey in life.

Thanks go out to Jody Colvard, for helping me with woman pod casting and getting my message out there to the world, for also being an inspiration to me.

Thank you to Dr.Harry and Andrea from Signature Eye Care in Brookfield, WI, for letting me adorn your "hip" frames on my bald head and for being your spokesperson.

Thanks to Jodie Lynn and the Parent to Parent Adding Wisdom Award, for giving HEADLINE IT! The most UNIQUE and BEST PRODUCT of 2006-2007, and the BEST CHILDREN'S HEALTH AND WELL BEING AWARD . Thanks for giving this book BEST BOOK OF THE YEAR award, as well. We humbly accept and thank you very much for the recognition of the value of our product and my book.

Thanks again to all the businesses, family members and others who helped make my dreams come true and for your continued support.

Many thanks to the cancer and alopecia patients that have worked with me over the years.

Most of all, I thank God for finding and inspiring me and for placing so many wonderful people in my path to call family and friends.

DEDICATED TO:

God
For giving every good thing

My parents, Fred and Karen
For their enduring love and support

My daughter, Jessica Ann
For unconditionally listening and loving

In memory of Grandma Marge
(1912-2004)
For touching our hearts forever

Alopecia and cancer survivors and those who suffer

"I have learned from experience that the greater part of our happiness or misery depends on our dispositions and not on our circumstance."
—*Martha Washington*

BALD IS BEAUTIFUL

Chapter One

Fish lake

IT WAS SUMMER at Fish Lake. I was daughter of the wind, a spirited updraft swooshing through tall pines and stands of hardwoods; a freckle-cheeked fish with long golden fins, swimming among perch, bluegills and muskellunge in cool dark places. Hot days kept me in and on the water and cool nights found me above it, laying on my back at the end of the pier with Rick, my brother, tracking orbiting satellites and wishing outlandish things upon shooting stars.

Ten thousand years ago this area was covered by Glacial Lake Grantsburg. Through time, it drained away leaving the deepest pockets of Fish Lake around thirty feet. The wind still carried faint whispers of the Fox, Dakota and Chippewa Indians that lived here before white settlement. Over thousands of years, Mother Nature simultaneously destroyed and healed this land and in my time generously endowed it with cranberries, blueberries, wild rice, water fowl, and wildlife of every kind.

I was a child of the outdoors and linked deeply to this place. There was order here, an order and language I understood and loved.

My mother's aunt discovered the lake first and bought a house on its shore. As a young girl, Mom visited her and satisfied her early love of horses by helping out at the stables nearby in exchange for an occasional ride. Later, when my parents were dating, they drove up from the city on weekends. It was accessible. And it was romantic. They married and brought us along from the time we were in diapers.

A local man approached my father one night at a bar. "Fred, I've got about twenty acres with lots of good lake frontage that I want to sell. I'm looking for some young Wisconsin couples, not Illinois, couples with children that love this place as much as I do and want to buy in cheap."

That was it. My parents met the criteria and flanked themselves with close friends on one side, my Uncle Jim and his family on the other. Together, they owned an impressive stretch of beach that everyone called Pliszka's Playground.

Our playground and the Fish Lake Wilderness in general, was a sanctuary where things with wings and fins and four legs outnumbered those of us with only two. The sun shined on it all, and time moved differently. As children, our days began when the light was too bright and the jays were too loud to sleep. Or, when the urge to play was so great, we couldn't resist it further. Nightfall came late with ghostly silhouettes, with loons and moons, and crayfish hunts.

Gone for three months were the hectic schedules, the need to succeed. Gone were the great expectations that made me crazy and made me bite my nails. Fish Lake. There was no place else I would rather play and relax than right here.

Things were set in motion that summer that changed my world. It began when my mother braided my hair. Long and blond, it was my trademark, the thing people first noticed about me.

We came home from the lake mid-week for Mom to do laundry and bookkeeping for Dad's business. I was outside with two of my friends when she called me in. It was hot that day, the hottest day all summer, and she wanted to make some small concession for the heat. It's what mothers do.

"Won't you be more comfortable if I braided your hair? Let's get it off your neck and shoulders. It'll make you feel cooler."

"Sure Momma." I was compliant and sat down in the kitchen with just enough restraint for her to do her job. She enjoyed the work. I wouldn't have been able to put it into words then, but I think my hair was as much a source of joy for her as it was for me. A sort of mutual pride. Later, when the tangles would take new shapes, when the snags simply got bigger, she remained consistent. She was always good with knots.

"Ouch!" She used the brush first to get the tangles out, then the comb. "Ouch. Mom, that hurts!" I knew not to protest too much. Doing so only made her hurry, and when she hurried she pulled harder.

"Sorry, Sweetie. Try to hold still. I'm about to get it."

The snarl relaxed and she brushed for a while, and as she did, all the swiftly moving parts inside me slowed to an amble. They always did. There was just this nice warm chemistry whenever mom did anything to my hair. I could feel it in the rhythms and in the stroke of her brush.

I jolted myself from this reverie. Now wasn't the time. "Please hurry, Momma. I need to get back out there." She took up a comb to work my hair into braids. Starting at the crown of my head, she pulled the tip of the comb gently downward. With a sudden catch of breath the spell was broken. I turned around looking at her.

"What's wrong?"

Calmly, she told me what she saw, "There is a small bald spot, the size of a quarter in the middle of your scalp."

"What?"

Going no further with the braids, Mom said, "Let's go to the bathroom and get a better look at what's going on here." I wanted to see the spot for myself. When she held up the mirror, I wasn't sure what I was looking at. Of course there was no answer when I asked her what it might be. She was as puzzled as I was. But she gave nothing away, and if there was any alarm in her voice, I didn't know it.

I spent a split second wondering if there really was anything to worry about. And I wondered if this discovery triggered her phobia about cancer. I had frightened them already with a fast-growing tumor behind my left eye when I was very young. She told me about it once. Through the miracle of prayer and a radical surgery that made medical news, my sight was saved and I was spared from the threat of cancer. Let's hope this wasn't as serious.

She then suggested a pony tail instead of braids. It was a small act, but one that would grow in time. Not long after, as I began to learn the subtle art of disguise for myself, as I became skilled at the art of camouflage, I turned to invention and creativity for my comfort. I was just beginning to notice mirrors, as you do at that age. I carried a comb with me wherever I went and kept it in constant motion when my hair hung loose. Every hair had its place.

I went back to my friends, back into the heat of that summer afternoon, and thought little about it.

My parents talked that night. "I have no idea what this could be, Fred. It bothers me. I put her hair in braids almost every day and I've never seen it before. What if it's cancer?

"Try not to worry and jump to conclusions. Maybe her ponytail was too tight and pulled some of the hair out. She's combing it all the time, maybe she's irritated her scalp. Maybe she got bit by something at the lake. I don't know, but I'm sure everything will work itself out."

"You're right. But you have no idea how much this has been eating at me all day long. I called a dermatologist near Southgate, I'm taking her tomorrow."

⌘⌘⌘

My parents took me to Palmer G. Tibbetts, M.D., the first of many doctors in our little story. A well known dermatologist, he was also a very nice man, an older man who took the time to make me feel welcome. This made it easier for me when he realized that his final diagnosis was that he had no diagnosis, that he wasn't at all sure what the problem was.

During my examination, I couldn't help but notice the odd look of his own scalp. The little stalks and shoots, the soft weedy sprouts. Perhaps I was already developing a certain curiosity for heads. He had hair plugs. Vanity is a strange master.

After examining my scalp closely, he still could make no conclusions. "It could possibly be an allergic reaction, or it might be any number of things." Either way, it was beyond his practice. He gave us the names of an endocrinologist and an allergist. The tests they conduct might bring better results. Before leaving his office he gave me a Halog solution and instructions on how to use it. I was to rub this on the bald spot three times a day.

Within a few weeks of using the solution, there was hair growth once again. Needless to say, my parents and I were relieved. I was ecstatic. A year passed and I was "spot free." The confidence that had been shaken during that first major skirmish, was fully restored. At thirteen you have raw belief on your side. The pitch of teenage life can work in your favor. The currents are swift, with many distractions. And some memories, as new as they might be, can be lost among them. But, home life was stable. My brother Rick and I were comfortable siblings by all outward appearances. I was one of the fortunate ones. Home was a source of support.

There was also a new intensity to my competitive life. Not only in sports, the basketball, and the track, but in my studies as well. I'm not sure how much any of this was connected to the image shock that I suffered, my desperate need to appear shining and perfect in my mother's eyes. I couldn't name it then, but I think I was jealous of the love she and Rick shared. I was certain that she loved him best. I had to out-do him to be seen. And so, my agenda grew. With everything else I was involved in, I was also in the choir, and was taking voice lessons at the time. I filled all my time with action, with a certain driven force beyond my years.

Chapter Two

His Sympathies Were Sweet

ONE DAY I was home combing my hair in front of the mirror, thinking of nothing, thinking of everything. And there it was again. Another bald spot, just to the left of my part, down the center. It was barely visible, but something in my heart deflated. I wanted to hide this discomfort from my parents and pretend like everything was all right, but couldn't. The spot was bigger than I was. I was still very young in this. It would season with me.

My mom walked past the bathroom door and saw me standing there, paralyzed, and staring helplessly into the mirror. I'm sure the tears gave me away as well. Without a word spoken between us, she just knew. Being older, being a mom, I suppose, being wise and cautious, she never lost the memory of that first offense. She kept it for both of us. I was too young. I had more resilience, more bounce perhaps. She had lived for at least a year with the suspicion of its return. She walked into the bathroom casually, not to set off any unnecessary alarms. She held me tightly and spoke to me with the assurance and warmth I needed. Our embrace was long and tender, and I could say nothing.

The fear that had gone quiet had come back. The next day, we were back in the dermatologist's office (Dr. Tibbetts). We tried the same treatment as before, this time with little success. I soon found myself in an allergist's office, Dr. Jacobson. The tests were long and painful. Puncture, prick, scratch, the usual torments. The next day we got the results.

"You're allergic to cats, dust, pollen, and the normal hay fever type allergies. Nothing unusual," he said. A special "health food" diet was prescribed. "If she could detoxify," he reasoned, "it might give sufficient shock to the system and heighten the immunities."

I had to drink goat's milk and eat alfalfa sprouts, among other things. There was nothing much that didn't taste like dirt. At fourteen, or at any age, this is not the typical fare nor was it chic. The goat's milk smelled so musky and foul that it actually made me throw up on the kitchen table. Mom decided this might not be quite the treatment for her daughter.

Soon, another bald spot appeared, this time over my right ear. I would say that the mere thought of the next treatment, looking back as I am now, makes my hair stand on end, but I haven't got any. *Cortisone shots*. I should have paid better attention when the doctor used the phrase "fairly painless" to describe the treatments.

The first battery was given in the hip. As he went about his work, I stared at the top of his head where all the budding vegetation was. This treatment didn't work either. We repeated it again and again, but after two months time there was still no re-growth on my head. Nothing.

Looking in the mirror at the large bald spot spreading around my ear, all I could do was cry. Crying was the only response I had at that time, at least the only visible one. The rest of it was inside me, all tangles and knots. Mom took a comb and fixed my hair in such a way that the spot was no longer visible. Another temporary fix, but it worked. And I had become the student. If I couldn't make it go away, I could hide it. I could pretend, make-believe.

Back at the dermatologist's office. Doctor Tibbets, sterilizing the bald spot with a swab of alcohol. This time the shots were going directly in my scalp, as if some direct attack, some last resort offensive was the only way. When he gave me the first shot, I couldn't help myself. I slammed my legs down on the table, and with real violence. Tears just weren't sufficient. But there was a lot you could do with a healthy pair of legs. And I could tell by the color draining from my mother's face that she wasn't taking this quite too well herself. She had a terrible fear of needles, and the sight of blood seeping into my hair put her near the edge. The pain was unlike anything I had felt before. The doctor injected my scalp again. And again. The paper beneath my head was wet with tears.

When he finished, I felt some small relief. Small. Then he turned my head to expose the bald area above my ear. It is a soft delicate area, nerve sensitive. He began the injections again, and something in me detonated. My feet lifted off the table. I slammed down hard with each pinprick. Of course, he informed me that tensing up was only making it worse. And of course, I didn't care.

Finally, I was done for the day. Doctor Tibbetts kept wiping the areas with cotton, and with each touch, I winced. I wanted to scream, but I couldn't scream loud enough. I couldn't cry hard enough. There was no satisfaction, no calming of my rage. As I sat up from the table at last, I felt nauseous and lightheaded. He gave me a lotion called Diprosone, to apply several times a day. I was half listening. The torment was over and I wanted to go home. My scalp began to swell and was still bleeding slightly. For days I couldn't sleep on that side.

I actually prayed for this treatment to work. I would gladly trade a small patch of hairless scalp for one small miracle.

After two weeks or so, I felt a little fuzz growing into the area. A small grove. I had to return to the doctor's office three weeks later for more shots. In spite of the distractions of my increasing nausea, and the anxious tedium of returning visits, the doctor explained certain things to my mom that I heard clearly. It was the first time I heard the word "alopecia."

"Based on my past experience, patients that have bald spots near the hairline areas like the temples or in the very front or back of the scalp, have a poor prognosis."

That was me.

"This is worst form of alopecia, and will result in more hair loss." He went on to explain that there are three types. Alopecia Areata (area) occurs when the body produces too many white blood cells, and white blood cells kill off infections. This was the type I presently had.

He said, "Your white blood cells think that your hair is an infection, and kills it off." With Areata, it takes only small patches of hair at a time. Sometimes the hair will grow back, sometimes not.

The next is Alopecia Totalis (total). With this condition, the patient loses all the hair on the head, and most of the facial hair as well.

The last form is the most severe. It is called Alopecia Universalis (universal). This condition exists when the body rejects all hair, even nasal hair. This is what I would eventually suffer.

I covered up my spots, an exercise I was getting more and more efficient at, and went into the waiting room while mom paid the bill. I was sore. I felt like I had just been beaten up, and by a medicine man. I felt alone. When we got home that day I went right to my bed. I was not only nauseous, but I felt as if I was in a trance. My brother, Rick, came into my room with his arm behind his back, hiding something from me. I looked at him and just started crying. He sat down on the edge of the bed, and without saying a word, pulled out a small stuffed polar bear. He handed it to me and gave me a hug. He said, "I wish it was me and not you having to go through all of this." His sympathies were sweet. They were immediate. It was his first response.

Because we were a family, we all had to find our way around this. It wasn't going to go away. My condition took on a presence of its own. It was difficult to avoid. Later, as I gave it more attention, it would grow. It would become large and cumbersome among us. Each of us had to search ourselves for new responses, for a new language, a new way of expressing. We had to find a mercy that was flexible and resilient. In the early stages of it all, there was warmth enough and hope enough and optimism enough to medicate our entire household. They'd rally around the threatened child.

Chapter Three

Perfect

SUMMER AGAIN. At last the burden of school lifted, it was time for us to go to the lake. It's what we did every summer. Fish Lake and the cottage that my dad built with his own two hands. The wide deck with the tall pine growing up through it. My room on the lowest level with its door to the path that led to the lake. The water, the wind. It didn't get any better than this. Dad stayed home during the week to run his roofing business, and drove up on the weekends. The rest of us were free to play and be ourselves.

Friends of my parents and their children had a cottage on one side of us and my Uncle Jim and his family were on the other side. My cousins were thin and petite, not very athletic like me. I had become an observer of these things in people. I noticed their eyes, hair, types and shapes. While not uncommon for adolescence, even normal perhaps, my need to judge went further than that. It came from a deeper place but I wouldn't know it yet.

Freed from the car, I ran in the cottage, threw open my suitcase, and riffled through all my stuff until I found my swim suit. I put it on, grabbed my towel, and ran out the door.

"Come on Rick. Hurry up." There was no need to explain. I ran for the beach, reckless and barefooted, the way life was supposed to be. I threw my towel down, ran as fast as I could to the end of the pier, and jumped in the water.

"Can you see them?" I asked him. Rick swam up next to me, and gave me a quick once-over.

"You're okay." I needed to know about the bald spots. I was carrying this weight with me everywhere now. Even in my play life. If he did see a spot, he managed to fix it for me the best he could. Fortunately, our days were mostly incident free.

The injections went on for several months, and the spots eventually closed themselves over with real hair.

"The pain had been worth it," I thought. I was perfect again. Just like our summer, perfect and complete. I grew quite an affinity for that word, *perfect*. I began to use the word a lot. It filtered into my thoughts, my judgments, the assessments I made of things around me. It actually scared me. So much that I kept it near me, making almost an idol of it. I had to be the best. I had to be perfect.

I took this belief back to school with me. I made the swim team and diving team. My favorite dives were the two-and-a-half forward tuck, and the reverse one-and-a-half. I worked hard to be the best diver I could be, the best swimmer. Again, to be perfect.

31

I love the water. I always have, since early childhood. Now I was concerned about my bald spots showing. There was no Rick to protect me, but I couldn't give it up. I hoped the spots would disappear under my thick hair.

During this time, I also had braces on my teeth. I had been wearing them for quite some time and was to have them removed within weeks. In spite of a few nasty spills at practice, I was winning diving meets and doing well at school.

We had a meet with West Allis Hale High School. After arriving, and after a time of warm-up in the pool, I headed over to the board to test it out. I waited my turn, and when it was time, gave the board a few good bounces. It seemed a bit loose to me, and I knew I would need to adjust to this. Also, there was something odd about the shape of the pool itself. I couldn't place it. I bounced higher and then higher and then higher again, and did a simple front flip forward.

The meet was underway and we were all ready to dive. I was on the side, stretching, waiting for my turn. I was prepared to do a fairly simple opening dive, a forward one-and-a-half flip in pike position. When it was finally my turn, I climbed up the ladder with my usual confidence. The way to reduce the splash on a dive is to enter the water in a very straight perpendicular position, and come as close to the board as possible without touching it. While I love track and swimming, that's all gross motor activity, pure guts and adrenaline. Diving is different. It's about finesse.

32

I saw the dive in my head, took a deep breath, and moved toward the end of the board. I performed a perfect dive. (How I loved that word.) I entered the water a straight line and very close to the board. This was going to get me a lot of points. I made contact with the water. I closed my eyes and felt that sense of rapture you feel when you know you've achieved something great. And though such a feeling is bigger than points, I loved the points. But all of this bliss was suddenly and violently interrupted with a crash. I somehow misjudged the depth of the pool and hit the bottom with my face.

I remember hearing this "crunch" sound, like someone had taken a bone and snapped it under water. My head and neck were compressed with such sudden violence, the pain was unbearable. My mind was clear enough to understand that since I could move, my neck wasn't broken. After all this, and while still submerged, my strongest thoughts were about my teeth. I was afraid I might have just lost some. I pushed to the surface and held my mouth while I escaped the pool. People were actually cheering for me, for my perfect dive. They had no clue what had just happened. That is, until they saw the blood. I had my perfect dive, and as great as that was, I didn't care. My teeth, my appearance, and the delicate balance of my vanity were at stake. They were as big as the applause and the perfect dive.

I walked along the side of the pool still holding my mouth in place, leaving a trail of blood behind me. I was obsessed with one thing, and that was to make it into the locker room to check my teeth. Jeannie, my swim-team friend, followed me and my crimson trail into the locker room. I was looking in the mirror crying, "My teeth! I can't lose my teeth!" After calling for an ambulance, my coach examined my mouth. The brace was broken, my chin and lips were cut badly and a tooth was loose but she was fairly sure that I wouldn't lose it. Other than that and an odd bruise that was getting brighter, I was alright.

I was in some degree of shock. I remember very little but I do remember that my dives weren't over and I was torn between finishing them and caring for my teeth. I became insistent about going back out. At least I think I did. I didn't, of course. Soon the ambulance was there. They put warm blankets around me and drove me to the hospital. I had ten stitches in my chin and several in the area around my lip. As sad-looking as I was, all I could think about was my teeth. I was told it was my braces that actually saved them. All that remained was a white looking scar on my chin and several on my lip area. A few weeks after my braces were repaired, they were removed. I was spared the indignity of being toothless.

I went back to diving practice, but something had changed. I was spooked. I developed a real aversion for the springboard. My dives suffered. Perfection had lost its initiative, lost its own teeth. I tried to rally, and I suppose I did, but that was the end of my diving career. I still hold the record number of points won for seven and eleven dives. And my coach still tells the story to her classes about the girl who was determined to finish. Track looked a lot safer to me now.

And singing. I'd been working toward diva since I was a little girl, singing in choirs and barber shop quartets, competing at many levels. My alto voice was perfected. With my greatest fan club, Mom, Dad and Grandma, in the audience, I walked off stage winner of state level competitions, and once won the Junior Miss talent contest. Singing was satisfying. I hadn't thought about the safety of it until my voice got hoarse.

I was sixteen years old. More spots appeared and then disappeared. It seemed like a cruel joke, but I took what I could get. I had a boyfriend. Brian. He was a good guy. Whenever I needed help with my feelings, which were becoming more and more complicated even to me, I could turn to Brian.

Graduation was approaching and I applied to several different colleges with track scholarships. I was excited about the prospect of going away to school. Still, I wanted to attend a college close to home. I had my reasons. One of which was Brian. I had an offer with a third class scholarship to run track at the University of Wisconsin Oshkosh. It was close to home, and yet far enough away to enjoy some independence.

I graduated from high school with a shoulder-length, sun streaked bob under my mortarboard. I didn't care that it was bought at the price of pain. I continued to live on the small hope that it was all over, that I had been victim of some adolescent affliction, like pimples. I told myself anything I needed to tell myself.

I took the offer at UW Oshkosh and while there I connected with a dermatologist, and by some good fortune, was "spot free" again for another two years. I was handling the injections better by now. It was a small price to pay for the salvation of my vanity. I had learned some biofeedback techniques of slowing my breathing down a bit, relaxing with pain. And though I'm sure it worked for some people, it didn't work at all for me. Neither did my longevity with Brian. I started dating someone else, a young man with a pilot's license and a plane at his disposal.

The hoarseness in my voice was still there. It was polyps. They'd been there for a long time and needed to come out. Surgery ended any thoughts this college freshman had of a singing career. Like diving, I tried, but it was no use. I'd find something else, another path, but not right now.

My grades were little better than average at this point. Having a good time began to mean more to me than scholastic achievement. My image of being best and beautiful was still my issue, of course; I just wouldn't let myself admit such a thing.

Chapter Four

The Accident

THE FIRE ALARM was the hottest dance club around. It was twenty minutes away in Appleton, another college town, and it was where we thought the most progressive kids hung out. Tomorrow I'd be twenty and tonight I was ready to party. Of course, when you're away at college, you didn't need much of an excuse to party. Still, it was my birthday. Mom and Dad would drive to Oshkosh around noon, but tonight Erik and I were going dancing, along with my best friend, and a few others.

With the exception of a few strobe lights that gave the room a pulse, it was a dark place, with lots of atmosphere. There were two dance floors and a DJ who played the best dance music around. Drinks were cheap anyway, but being my birthday, my drinks were free. Actually, I didn't drink at all, but offered mine to whoever wanted it. Helen, my best friend, didn't drink either. We downed diet coke with lemons, and proved that outrageous and silly is not limited to the intake of alcohol.

Erik drove a big Cadillac. It was old and white. Like Moby Dick, I thought. It was a legend around campus. We piled in and took the lead. Helen, her boyfriend Pare, and another couple were following in a car behind us. "Purple Rain" blasted on the radio, and music from a Norwegian group, AHA, who had once lived down the street from Erik before he left for college. We sang along like a band of twenty, but there were only three of us in the car, Erik, me, and my cousin, Lynn.

We exited the highway and were making our way around Appleton city limits when Erik suggested a detour. Who cared? I mean, does danger actually have a smell? Didn't *party* always come before *precaution?* I was still reveling on a non-alcoholic high. I jumped out at the four-way stop and ran toward Helen's open window. "Hang a right. We're taking a short cut," I yelled. It was freezing outside. I shuddered, got back in the car, and slammed my passenger door as the wheels began to turn. I twisted around to talk to Lynn in the back seat. Then it happened. As the unexpected can when you're in a moving vehicle, it came with a loud crash, metal on metal.

We spun around violently. The impact threw me right-arm first into the dashboard. My seatbelt couldn't help me because I wasn't wearing it, and there was nothing to prevent my being thrown forward. I grabbed at anything that would slow me down. Like the ashtray. It made as much sense as anything else. This was just before my head hit the windshield with a spandex-like give before shattering the glass. The rest of me was on the floor wedged under the dash. Things went dark.

The next thing I remember were the red, white, and blue lights. They reflected on the broken glass that was everywhere, and made an eerie sparkle. I saw the accelerator, the brake, and the dislodged ashtray as I regained my senses. There were voices; near, far, men, women. There was a siren. And pain, lots of pain.

A fireman was prying and reaching, talking softly in a courteous and professional voice. A paramedic informed me that I had three dislocated fingers, which he swiftly jammed back into place. I yelled, and the effort seemed to split my head open. I was laid out on a stretcher and moved into the rear of a waiting ambulance. Lynn held my hand during the ride. She was much more fortunate than I and tried to rally my spirits by making light of this odd birthday turn of events. I tried to ask questions, but wasn't making much sense. Everything was a blur. I couldn't sort it all out. Lynn said something about a carload of sixteen-year olds signaling one way and turning another. And the sudden and unavoidable U-turn, the one that turned nasty. We hit them broadside. "Everyone is okay, except you, and you're going to be fine," she assured me. I let myself believe every word.

The emergency room lights were bright and sterile, as they usually are, and I was shivering. I was given a thermal blanket. People scurried about and whispered short orders. I felt an urgency to call my parents and let them know I was all right, but didn't. Glass was removed from my hair and scalp. They took x-rays and stitched up my hand. I had a concussion. I also suffered muscle and tissue damage on the right side—cuts, bruises, and some questionable issues with two spinal vertebrae. I would need to spend the night for observation.

Before being wheeled to a room, I met with Lynn and the others. The young girls from the other car were with them. Their eyes were full of concern and relief. Considering I was still alive, that I was in one piece, the apologies they made and the consolation they offered me were indeed sweet. I mumbled something, some warm benediction I'm sure, and drifted off to sleep.

Chapter Five

Surprise

THE HOSPITAL RELEASED ME mid-morning on my birthday. Helen and her boyfriend picked me up. I stretched out on the back seat with my head on a pillow behind Pare so I could see and talk with Helen. Pare drove carefully, cornering wide, avoiding abrupt stops, barely creeping over railroad crossings. I was glad to see this side of him, the considerate side, especially since Helen told me she thought she was falling in love.

I limped between the two of them to my room in Scott Hall. "Yes, I'll be fine. No, I don't need a thing other than a quiet day to recover." As soon as the door closed behind them, I made a bee-line for bed, the little twin with its brick-hard mattress. I never thought I'd appreciate a bed so much. I kept my shoes and jacket on, found a comfortable position on my back, and closed my eyes.

The key turned in the lock. It was Linda, my roommate. We didn't know each other well, but she was quiet. She was respectful of my space and at the sight of me, rushed over and asked what was wrong. I told her about the accident. I told her that I had just come from the hospital and felt like crap. She asked me if I needed anything, any assistance, and I gracefully declined. She left the room to study in the lounge. Again, the blessed door closed. I slept, and dreamed. The echoes were brutal, but distant. I heard the sound of metal against metal. I heard voices. I began spinning. Then there was nothing.

⌘⌘⌘

Bang! Bang! Bang! Someone's fist was pounding on my door. I sat up, disoriented, and stumbled my way over. The pounding came again and it hurt my head. It was a friend telling me I needed to come quickly to Helen's house. "Quickly" was hardly a word you'd find in my vocabulary at the moment. And even against my small resistance, or the pitiful sight I must have made, she seemed excited, persistent. Something happened to Helen and she needed me. Without a word, I closed the door and shuffled along side her, down the block.

Things looked in order. There were no ambulances, no fire trucks. I took that as a good sign. After a light knock on the door, it flew open to a thunderous "SURPRISE! HAPPY BIRTHDAY, JODI!" I saw stars, and felt myself tilt backwards. I thought I'd pass out, but instead, I smiled in my delirium, and walked through the door into a room full of well wishers.

Surprise, all right. The sight of me was the real surprise. "Had I gone ten rounds with a prize fighter or what?" I felt like it.

My parents were in the middle of the room. The sight of my injuries brought more emotion to their eyes than I could handle. I moved toward them and they embraced me. I wept at the comfort of having them near. Despite the miles between us, I was still very much their little girl and it was as necessary for me to tell them what had happened as it was for them to hear it. I knew we'd be fine when Dad said, "Good thing you have a hard head!" It was his special gift, the one he pulled out when the occasion demanded it. We shared the laugh and turned our attention to the party.

There was laughter, music, food, and a room full of caring friends. I was exhausted from the excitement, and after thanks and goodbyes, I left with my parents to their hotel room where a queen-sized bed was waiting for me.

The following morning my parents were sitting by the window reading the paper when I opened my eyes. I had slept well in the safety of their presence once again. My neck was stiff and sore, but that was to be expected. I was still grateful that I had escaped with so much of me intact.

I pried myself out of bed and turned to straighten the covers when I noticed something on my pillow. I felt the old sting of recognition. I stiffened, not wanting to believe what I was looking at. I wanted to scream, but sat down on the bed and stared out the window, beyond my parents. My mother took one look at me and left her chair. She saw it and said a soft, "Oh no." Her arms folded around me. I leaned softly into her and became a little girl again. On the pillow was a large clump of my hair.

⌘⌘⌘

My body healed, and the bruises disappeared. But every shower became another torment. Every shampoo, however gentle my approach, claimed more hair. Shampooing less frequently didn't help either. On the way to the shower, I bargained with God. If he would let my hair stop falling out, I would change my life. He was silent. Nothing worked. The hair kept coming out. On the days I washed it, I made sure nobody else was around. The embarrassment of exposing my bald spots, even in a community shower where we were all somewhat vulnerable, was too great. This took some effort, and patience. I often made four or five attempts before finding the showers empty.

I can't remember feeling so helpless and destitute. In the shower, I rinsed gobs of hair off my fingers, and watched them cascade to the drain. I closed my eyes and leaned up against the wall, void of hope, of good will, void of all joy, or any promise of joy. The water flowed over me and I prayed. I bargained and I begged until I realized water was rising to my ankles. The drain was clogged with hair, my hair. I picked the soft mass off the drain cover and was wrapping it in a paper towel when another girl walked in. I dropped the hair on the floor and quickly made a turban with my towel. She looked at the thing on the floor, but said nothing. I hurried out.

Having achieved some degree of tunnel vision, and forgetting Linda was there and napping, I slammed our door. I wanted to hide, but there was nowhere safe. She woke and sat up. I mumbled some nonsense apology and headed for my side of the room.

"I've got to scoot. See you in a few hours," she said and was gone.

I approached the mirror, dropped the towel, and combed my hair, or what was left of it. A stranger looked back at me. Or something wild. "I don't know who you are. And I hate you. Go away."

I became the queen of the comb-over. That was me. I suddenly had empathy for old vain men. The more hair I lost, the more elaborately I twisted and turned the remaining strands. I plastered them in wavy rows and sections. I held everything in place with bottles of White Rain. I attached myself to any friend willing to view me from a hundred different angles to be sure no bald spots were visible. During bad weather, especially wind and rain, I begged rides to class rather than risk walking and being exposed by the elements. I was drunk with this. Out of control. I was ashamed of my own image, ashamed of what I was becoming. Except for Erik, and a few close friends, I kept this to myself.

I had lost so much hair there was no way to conceal it any longer. All my delight in perfection turned to loathing and with the identical strength. It's funny how that works. How perfection, or the dream of perfection, and vanity are so intimately acquainted, one with the other. And just how close rage lies beneath it all.

"I hate you! I hate you!" This was my new mantra. I was lost. Suddenly lost. *Mirror, mirror, on the wall, who's the fairest . . .* Oh, if this was only a fairy tale, it might promise me some happier ending. But I couldn't see one. I couldn't see much of anything. Only this savage lost thing in my mirror.

Disgust turned to fury. I jabbed the point of a rat-tailed comb into my scalp. "I hate you!" I jabbed until blood ran into my eyes. A shadow fell over my heart.

That Friday afternoon I dialed home. Mom answered. "Help me, please," I cried. "I can't take this anymore. I don't want to live this way." I never thought of calling anyone else, and no one else was ever as available to listen to me as my mother.

"You can't cover the spots anymore, right?" she asked. "Well, Honey, maybe it's time for a wig. I'll drive over in the morning. Expect me at ten o'clock."

"Are you nuts?" I thought to myself. *"Are you out of your mind? I wouldn't be caught dead wearing some stupid old-lady Grandma wig. I'm not wearing a wig, ever!"*

"Okay, Mom," I said. "See you at ten." I hung up the phone.

Chapter Six

My First Wig

MOM WAS AT MY DOOR precisely at ten o'clock in her typical "take charge and get it done" way. When I saw her, something in me sank. What must she be thinking? I felt ashamed, ashamed that losing my hair had let her down. I was a disappointment to her now, a burden, something less than a whole daughter. Perhaps she read my thoughts as she too put on a smile and took a deep breath.

"Come on. Let's go. Don't worry about a thing." She took me by the hand, her crippled child, and led me to the car.

Les Wigs Boutique, in Wauwatosa. It was reportedly the best wig shop in the state. The store entrance was flanked by two large display windows with tiers of red-lipped mannequins wearing all kinds of hair. *"Should I bolt?"* My mother held the door open. I entered a bit nervous, yet curious.

The shop owner greeted us. Mom had begun researching wigs the instant we hung up the day before. The two women chatted now like old friends. Lucene was robust and vivacious. She was gregarious, an extroverted woman, good for sales. Her hair was bright red with blonde highlights. "It's a wig," she volunteered, after I locked my gaze upon it.

"It's pretty," I said, looking away, hoping I hadn't been rude. I wasn't sure how to behave. I didn't want to be here. I felt resistance, but I had also cried out for help. Along with her bold wig, Lucene had excessively long and extravagantly painted nails. Her right pinkie was so long it curled up at the end. She read me reading her. She was warm and genuine, and she knew her stuff. She knew exactly what to say to me and how to say it.

Lucene educated us on the merits of man-made versus synthetic wigs. She continued with types of caps, wig construction, and cost. Wig after wig was brought out to us as she spoke. As time passed, so did my apprehension and my previous judgments. Lucene was so matter-of-fact about it all, as if it was the most natural thing in the world. She discussed quality, maintenance, comfort, and the security of wearing a wig. I felt everything but secure. I then hated this. My thoughts were wild with complaint and speculation. *"This is the point of no return. This is where I disappear forever under an itchy scratchy head of someone else's hair. Nothing will be left of the once-natural girl, the one with the beautiful hair. There will be no future, no swimming, running, long jumping. Who would date me? Who would want me? I will be artificial. The wig, a prosthesis, will remind me of what I am missing. I will be a freak."*

48

We made a decision at last. We left, filing past the rows of mannequins at Les Wigs Boutique. They were faceless, nameless, without substance, without feeling. They counterfeited real life and I was terrified that I would become one of them.

Chapter Seven

A break

IT WAS CHRISTMAS BREAK, my junior year at the University of Wisconsin Oshkosh. My boyfriend had gone back to Norway for the holidays, and without me. But it *was* Christmas, and the thought of going home became stronger than the disappointment of one guy's oversight. There was too much consolation waiting on me to be upset.

Rick would be there. I missed Rick. We had been close as children, even through high school. College changed him. Maybe it was the leaving home, having to find his own way in the world. He had a couple of rough years at a private school in Ripon, and then a brief stint at UW Oshkosh while I was there. His frustration with grades and other things I wasn't privy to, forced him to eventually drop out. He took a job as manager of a local bar. We lived in the same town, and yet there was a divide between us. He shunned me, as if it was too much to admit I was his sister. He seemed angry all the time. After reaching some saturation point, he simply left town with a UW classmate to work construction in Illinois. As odd as it was to me, this event, while creating havoc between Rick and my parents, served to reconnect the two of us. Siblings in exile. We began writing. His letters were long and loving. Still, I said little or nothing about losing my hair or how I felt about it. I was eager to see him again. We were all going to be together. Christmas has great medicine in it. At least I was hoping it did.

I pulled into my parent's driveway. The house was the same it had always been, with one exception—it had been weaned of our presence, swept clean of my brother and me. Our pictures were still there, but the personality of the house was all theirs, Mom and Dad's. In short time, we had become house guests as effortlessly as the two of them had become empty nesters. Still, it was great to be here. Absence had truly made my heart grow fonder.

Rick and I got up the next morning and set out boxes of ornaments to trim the tree. We both felt it, I guess. That old anticipation, that sleepless thing children of all ages feel, the thing that Christmas and homecoming does to the spirit. It was early. I was in my favorite flannel pajamas. I hadn't brushed my teeth yet and was enjoying my first sips of hot cocoa. Having slept with nothing on my head, I abandoned my usual practice of putting on my wig and a touch of makeup before coming out of the bedroom. The struggle with my vanity was already getting old, but it wasn't over. The gradual alteration of my appearance was demanding more and more of me.

In spite of the levity of morning, and in spite of the good will that woke with us at dawn, Rick couldn't look at me when we talked. His aversion was conspicuous. I had grown sensitive to these things and was struggling to gain some mastery over them. My antennae had grown sharp and quick. He developed a sudden fascination with the ornaments, and could not or would not put into words any thoughts he was having at the sight of his sister's patchy, mostly bald head.

The wig could have spared us both this discomfort. I wanted him to say something, anything, even something dumb. It would have to be better than the silence that had crept between us. Anything. He was my brother, after all! The suspense was unsettling. I had developed a large dislike for leaving things unsaid, things that can fester, metastasize beneath the surface. "There's an elephant sitting in our living room, but don't disturb it. And whatever you do, don't tell the neighbors." This was the unwritten rule in our house and probably most houses of parents from their generation. And it drove me crazy. Being as sensitive as I had become, I knew better than the rest of them the damage such a rule can cause. It was one household myth no one dared to challenge. It was a prison I didn't want to be in. I was considering the best way to open up a conversation with Rick when Mom came in.

"Jodi, why don't you put a scarf or something around your head when you aren't wearing your wig?" I stood there looking at her, voiceless and numb. By her facial expression I knew she was disappointed, bordering on disgust. *"How could you inflict yourself upon us like that?"* At least this was my perception of things. Shame can exaggerate the judgments we make, distort our assessment of things, things that help us order our world. I thought I heard it in her voice. I was no stranger to shame. My dignity suffered cruelly beneath its weight, and began to wither inside me. Like Rick's once-warm sympathies.

Suddenly the beautiful sleepy holiday morning had become something ugly and bitter. I had become something unpleasant and unacceptable to her, and, as was her style, she would rather it just go away, or at least hide itself. Right or wrong, those were my thoughts. Rick looked away. All the sweetness was purged from the morning—from the tree, from the house. I no longer felt an alliance with him. I was alone, and I could not repress my tears. They were the only comfort I had.

The two-week break stretched into forever. Everything had changed and I felt like an exile, trying to fit into the good graces of my own family. I did what was expected of me. I wore the wig. Choosing not to fight, I pampered all their illusions. Toward the end of the last week, with little or no provocation I would just start crying. I didn't know what to do with all this.

"Just get me out of here and back to school." Maybe it was a Christmas wish. It was too bitter and too lonely to be a prayer.

My parents had ideas of their own concerning my immediate future. My father approached me alone. He and my mother had been doing a lot of thinking, and they decided it would be best for me to take some time off from college. "We want you to come and live at home with us and maybe decompress. We just think you're too stressed out with all that's happening. We want you to come home and relax."

It was a generous offer, so like them, but to me it was unfathomable. I had one year of school left. I had a boyfriend, and I had a life of my own in Oshkosh. I couldn't just quit and come home. I knew the question to ask, the one that would release me. "You didn't raise me to be a quitter, did you Dad?" He didn't disappoint me. I knew him too well. I would not quit. I would survive.

Whether I wanted to admit it or not, I had some history with quitting. I quit the track team, giving up the anchor, or last leg position in the 440 relay, something I was good at. I just couldn't see running with a wig on. I quit walking to school because the wind blew what hair I had left and revealed my bald spots. My dad even bought me a car to compensate.

My condition ruled my life, in spite of my energies, in spite of the optimism that I forced to the surface at times. A month before Christmas break I left the dorm I was in to avoid embarrassment

54

of the community showers. I moved into my own apartment so I could be as bald as I was without fear of discovery, rejection, or ridicule. My life was shrinking, caving in on itself.

⌘⌘⌘

It was good to be back at school, back in the daily routine, into the swarm of life, being caught up on its currents and the continuing momentum of things around me. My boyfriend was back and all was well.

I preferred to study late at night. I hadn't realized the creativity it took just to live, to adapt, to discover ways to disguise my life, which was often just as barren as my scalp. There was comfort in the dim quiet of my living room, pages turning, my mind occupying itself with industry. My grades had been good so far.

I was cramming later than usual one evening for a psychology exam. At some point in the night I leaned over the table, removed my glasses and rested my head for a moment. When I opened my eyes again, I nearly shrieked at the black spider standing on my notebook. I was about to smash it when I realized it wasn't a spider at all. It was my eye lashes. I went to the bathroom mirror and studied the gap. I pulled lightly on the remaining lashes and as I suspected, more of them gave way. My heart sank, again. Within two days, my once-beautiful and perfect eyelashes were as much of a memory as the hair on my head.

Losing my eyelashes was just another wave, another blow to my appearance that put even more distance between me and *normal*. With each increment of loss, each new assault to my image, I had to adjust. And the adjustments were not so graceful either, but I had to push forward. I was continuously learning, unlearning, and relearning. Pushing my creativity and invention to new limits. This was no different.

My fear bordered on hysteria. I cried. I screamed. I railed against God. Again, I blamed him. I told him how much I hated him, then begged and demanded to know "Why me?" The night all of my eyelashes fell out, my boyfriend stayed, for support. Even so, I spent the night on the bathroom floor. It was hard and it was cold, wet with tears. The next morning, I got up and went to class, wearing sunglasses.

There was one pair of false eyelashes to a box. They were long and bushy. Trimming and thinning them was easy, but mastering the glue strip on my lash line was not. If they were crooked, which they often were in the beginning, I'd rip them off and start all over again. My lids were red and raw from the many false starts. My agitation didn't help. Like so many things, I got used to the pain and the inconvenience, and got better at applying them. Having eyelashes and hair, real or not, made me normal, at least the illusion of normal, which was sufficient. Between vanity, pain, humility, outrage, fear, all the elements that had bound and gagged me, it was difficult to distinguish one illusion from the next. "Normal" became a very elastic word. I was afraid of it. I gave it a lot of stretch.

⌘⌘⌘

One afternoon at the campus library, Erik and I ran into his old girlfriend. Introductions were made and my first thoughts were not that pleasant. She wasn't very attractive and I couldn't help but think she was shaped somewhat like a pear. I felt relief. And though that relief was based on my perceptions, perceptions of me, of who I was, as distorted and as grievous as those perceptions had become, it at least assured me that if he could date someone with a shape like that, my chances must be pretty good. My reason was contaminated like everything else, though I was unaware at the time. Image held the seat of power in my mind. It seemed to be the center around which all things revolved, the lens through which I began to see all life around me.

From the start, my boyfriend was different from the rest. His accent, his light blonde hair, and his large blue eyes set him apart. He was a scuba diver and a pilot. On weekends, and whenever we could, we flew, we danced, we bar hopped, grocery shopped, studied, and visited my parents. I hoped the sight of my father's

944 Porsche assured him that my family was as well off as his own. At that time, such things were important to me.

We had been at the library for a good hour when I excused myself and headed to the restroom. I passed a lecture hall. The door was open and I spotted a friend in the front row. I slowed my pace and we exchanged a quick wave and when I looked away from her, the ex-girlfriend I'd just met stood directly in front of me in the hallway. She came in fast and close, looked me squarely in the eye. "I hate you. You took him away from me, you bitch!" she hissed. Without missing a beat, and with something crude and indiscernible under her breath, she reached for my wig, jerked it from my head, and threw it into the same lecture hall which just happened to be full that day.

I stood there bald and exposed before a hundred pair of eyes, when the devil in me was loosed. I looked at them and then looked at her. I knocked her down and grabbed her hair. I held her hair in one hand and beat her senseless with the other. I whaled and pounded. She tried to shield her head, but there was no defense. The violence in me was too large, too dominant. Something inside me snapped. I had no restraints. All my nerve flushed forward. I was overtaken with energy beyond my own strength, some combination of adrenaline and wrath. All this rage pent up in me from years gathered together against this poor girl who had no idea the storm she had just liberated. I felt out of my body for a while then I heard voices and felt someone pull me off. All tension stilled and I was aware again.

Chapter Eight

Tangles

I COULDN'T PUT THE THING ON MY HEAD or get my eyelashes just right without emotion, without feeling something, usually resentment. I was the one tangled in all this hair. Human hair, synthetic hair, hair-burned-up-on-the-radiator-trying-to-dry-it hair, one-disaster-after-another hair, and hair that wasn't even there.

With time, my complaints lessened. The human-hair wigs looked almost like my own, sun-streaked and golden blond. No one on campus seemed to even notice, partly because I sat in back of class, came late, left early, and gave them no chance to. My close friends saw my new hair and were gracious. I could only hope they were telling me the truth. I shampooed my wigs. I hot-rolled them, styled them, and dried them on lava lamps or anything else that protruded enough to hold them. When they wore out and started getting bald spots of their own, I applied my father's ingenuity by cutting them up and meticulously hand-sewing pieces of one to the other.

To me, the biggest curse of wearing a wig was the damper it put on fun at the cottage. Summers were hot, and I was part fish. I needed to be in the water. I always had been. But not now, I wouldn't swim at all. I was positive that if I wore a wig in the water, it would come loose and float off. The thought of me swimming after it was more than I could bear. And, I was too embarrassed to expose my bare head. Being bald was too new to ask anyone else to accept, I hadn't accepted it yet myself. So I wore the wigs. I sweated and got rashes on my scalp. I waded around the shore and dangled my legs off the end of the pier. All the joy and memory of summer melted away and I wondered if I'd ever want to return.

My world compressed somewhat. My social life became guarded. There were few I cared to confide in about any of this. Helen Nelson was the only person I could talk to it seemed. She had problems of her own, and together we found mutual comfort.

I guess you could call this my "black era." My thoughts were black, or gray enough to look black. The clothes we wore were all black and the feeling we felt against the world was black, too. I had an ally in Helen. I was trying to be happy, but I was miserable, exchanging all my color for black. I rejected God. He disappeared in my background. My soul was in need of repair, I'm sure. Helen was a Christian, and she wasn't afraid to talk about her faith. I just chose not to listen.

My changing disposition did not go unnoticed by my parents. They drove up often to check on me, to take my temperature, to rescue me. They had their ways and knew what melted me. Once they surprised me with a kitten. She purred too sweetly and was too soft to refuse. Fluffy spent her first weekend with Helen and me fussing over her; that is, until I started coughing and wheezing and struggling for breath. "Help, I'm having an asthma attack!" I called to Helen. "But I don't have asthma." She hurried me to the Emergency Room where I was reminded that I was allergic to cats. With the hair gone from my nose, nothing was being filtered. Dust, fur, dander, it all went directly to my lungs. Fluffy left before I was ready to let her go. I missed her.

Helen and I picked up where we left off pre-Fluffy. We had fun going out, and I even dated here and there. Dating and being intimate with guys made me feel a sense of security, even if it was a false one. Looking back, it was all filler. Like jelly in a donut. No real substance or worth. Sweet, but with no real benefit to the health. I was empty and found myself depending on others for some sense of myself, depending on them to fill that part of me that seemed bankrupt. I couldn't figure out why I was always angry and upset, but I knew wearing this wig made me feel like a different person, a person I decided I didn't like.

Then I met T. J. He was actually a twin of a man that I went to school with. He was visiting his brother. Once we connected, conversation came easy. "Don't I know you?" I said. "You look familiar." He walked up closer to me and said, "I don't know you, but I'd like to." I blushed and continued flirting. "My brother goes to UW Oshkosh. I'm his twin," he said. I had no hair, other than the wig I was wearing, no eyelashes, other than those I bought and pasted on, nothing to make me appear beautiful. But I had a nice figure and I could hold my own with intelligent conversation. I became a master of deception, a siren of sorts. It appeared to be working.

The flirtation was mutual, and it continued. It also yielded the desired result. Instinctually, I knew I could capture this guy under my spell with or without hair. Within a few weeks we were dating heavily. I had told him nothing about the wig, not yet. Several times he wanted to put his hand on the back of neck, but I wouldn't let him. My whole body was rigged with trip wires, it seemed. It was too big of a risk. I was sure he would be able to feel the back of my wig, and uncover the deception. Perhaps by now he had some curiosity about it. I don't know. He was unaware that I was wearing a wig at the moment, unaware of the bigger mystery of *why* I had to wear one. I had become quite proficient at hiding, at misdirecting. I told him it tickled when he touched me there.

Lying went with the territory. I was an actress now. My looks, my feeling about my looks, the rejection I felt from the mirror itself, the rejection I suffered at my own hand, lying was just easier, safer. Of course, it didn't feel like lying. It felt like self-preservation, survival.

I giggled like a school girl. I played hard-to-get and wouldn't allow him to touch my neck. This was a game I could do. It involved deception, acting, being elusive and not altogether truthful. Love and mystery go together, right? It made him feel playful, as if I was engaged in some rite of courtship, a maddening give and take. But I was just hiding my secret.

I never thought I would find a man to accept me for who I was until he came along. I began to believe that of him, anyway. For months, things seemed to be going well, he was a perfect gentleman, and his charm seemed to work on everyone, including me. We got along together famously and he seemed to genuinely care for me. Within just a few weeks it turned ugly.

One night, a night that seemed warm between the two of us, a night of soft conversation and what appeared to be trust, I decided to tell my story to T. J. I began with the accident. I told the whole story. There was a lot of room for sympathy in it. The negligence, the absence of my seat belt, the shattered windshield, the hospital, and so on. I started to cry. I worked up the courage to continue. The more I embellished the story, the better response I seemed to get from people. Still an actor's trade. He took my hands and looked into my eyes as I told my story. "Don't worry, I'm here for you," he said. "You can trust me, just tell me what happened." Actors with actors.

I told him about the condition, about the alopecia. I explained what I could, that basically my body produced too many white cells, that my hair looked to them like the enemy. That the white cells won. Each time I told my story, it was like a game. As I explained, I stepped around the truth somewhat, tiptoeing lightly around the awful revelation hidden under my wig. I always tried to read what the other was thinking before saying, "Hey, I'm bald!" I had to be sure it was alright to come out.

After going on and on, I asked T. J. if he understood what I was telling him. He looked at me rather puzzled, then said, "do you mean you don't have any hair?" I broke down and started crying uncontrollably. I was embarrassed and afraid that after he found out the truth he would leave me. He said nothing and put his arms around me. He then asked me, "How come you have hair now?"

I looked at him, and after a long pause said, "this isn't my real hair." I translated his look as amazement. "Remember how you always wanted to touch the back of my neck and I never let you?"

"Yes. It drives me crazy when you do that."

"I didn't want you to find me out. That's why I didn't want you to touch me there." My voice was quieter, softer now. I was exposed.

He said, "With all you were saying and building up, I thought you couldn't have kids or something, or you had your insides removed or something tragic, not just this." He made it sound minor. I was relieved. He was reacting positively. I took a deep breath and felt closer to him at that moment. This was "the one."

This was the man I was going to marry. "Who else would love someone like me?" I thought.

"I love you so much, Jodi. You know I am the only person that will ever love you. After all, who would want someone that looked like an alien in the morning with no eyelashes or hair?" My heart stopped. I couldn't believe what he just said to me. Could this be happening? He wanted to keep me for himself and would say whatever it took to make sure I would never leave him. He mixed good and bad in the same sentence. I felt like a queen and a toad all at once.

I had no experience with verbal abuse and didn't realize I was the recipient of it. As all successful predators do, he targeted my weakness. It worked. My countenance drooped with each assault. As women, we might tend to overlook things like this too often. We rationalize too well and too weakly, and accept what should be unacceptable. All my dissembling, all my fabrications, all my acting and affectations, all these things had sprung a trap, and I was the poor fox.

"You are so beautiful, Jodi, and it doesn't bother me that when you take your hair off you look like a freak." He actually said those things. I couldn't believe my ears. The words were in total contrast to the considerate and gentlemanly behavior he had shown me all along. And I wish I could say it ended there, but it didn't. Verbal abuse wasn't enough for T. J. It turned physical.

Sitting in the car one Christmas eve, T. J. got ruffled because we couldn't find a parking place. He yelled, "What kind of dump is this? Aren't there any damn parking spots? This pisses me off." He then hit me so hard in the face with the back of his hand my glasses went flying off.

"What the hell did you do that for?" I screamed. "You bastard, how dare you hit me!" My tears were now angry tears. At least I hadn't lost all my dignity, nor did I fall fawning beneath the weight of this offense.

"Shut up, bitch!" he yelled at me. His face was red with rage. His dad was an abuser. A retired police officer, he hit T. J.'s mother fairly regularly, and didn't care who saw it. T. J. was his father's son. Having no experience with such a thing, I never dreamed I'd be with such a person. Again, the deceptions led me here. His and mine. I have to believe that. A false path, a false love, and an unhappy ending.

At first I thought that I had to take the abuse. After all, who was ever going to love me? He had me brainwashed to that effect. As we entered my cousin's home, after finally finding a parking place, he threatened, "I will hurt you even worse if you tell your family what I did." I grabbed my purse, opened up the mirror on the visor, wiped away the tears, and took a deep breath. I was so embarrassed that I had allowed myself to get into this situation. I could never tell anyone what happened, or they would be angry with me. I felt imprisoned. I had nothing but my own thoughts to keep me company.

I put on a happy face and simply continued to do what I was really getting good at, deception. If I ignored things, or repressed them, maybe they would go away. Of course, they didn't. And of course, it just got worse. He proceeded to honeymoon me the entire evening, convincing my family with a show of charm. "Doesn't Jodi look pretty tonight? Am I not the luckiest man in the world."

I told my mom what happened between T. J. and me, but for some reason she didn't want to believe it. Either that, or she dismissed it as something I would have to handle for myself. I got angry with her. I don't want to spend much time on these events, but maybe something in this story will help those of you who suffer similar entrapments and emotional undertows.

The evening was a disaster for me. I spent a lot of time in the bathroom, pretending I wasn't feeling well. I kept crying and had to hide my pain somehow. I was paralyzed to act at all, particularly in the presence of my family. I was lost, as in a maze.

We left, finally, and T. J. dropped me off at home. "I am sorry that I lost my temper with you before, Jodi. There is a lot of stress at work and I guess that I just took it out on you. Please forgive me. I love you so much, and can't live without you. Please forgive me." He squeezed my hand tightly as he spoke. Without saying a word, I accepted his apology, letting myself believe it.

The abuse continued here and there, and T. J. would always beg forgiveness afterwards. This began to happen a bit too often.

"If you touch me one more time, T. J., so help me God, I am going to tell your mom, your dad, my parents, and I'm going to leave you! No more apologizing. Just stop the abuse!" Of course, he complied, and with all the right music in his voice, all the right facial cues.

I felt like this was just who he was, and maybe I could overlook the abuse. I deceived myself with that one. I began to loathe him, to slowly detach myself from him. My neediness was at stake. It got me here in the first place. But the abuse was unbearable. I put my neediness aside and knew deep in my heart I was going to have to leave him, I just needed to figure out how. I didn't want to live this way anymore. My parents taught me better than this, and I discovered I had much more self respect in me to continue this madness any longer.

I graduated from college on schedule and moved back home with my parents. I was even closer to T. J. We had dated nearly two years. That's how long my will had held up, the need for acceptance. But the price I was paying was way too much. Despondent much too often, I couldn't see a way out. This happens to many women, and doesn't mean these women aren't strong, only deceived, and trapped.

I was working as a counselor, and ironically listened to how a lot of women were being abused by their boyfriends and husbands. Luckily, an offer for a great counselor position (Great Expectations) in Ohio was offered to me. I took the job. I told T. J. I was moving.

He looked perplexed. "What did you say?" I told him again that I was moving to Ohio, that I wanted a new start, without him, and I hoped he would understand. Mixed with his begging me to stay he managed to call me a "bitch," a "bald-headed bitch" at that. He said I was "ugly" and "detestable." He finished this with "please stay with me!" That's how crazy this had become.

The venom in his words confirmed my decision. I told him goodbye, and that I never wanted to see him again. He grabbed a chair and threw it across the room. Then he came toward me with his fist raised in the air. Just then, my parents opened the door, and I ran towards them, and into my Dad's arms. My dad knew exactly what was going on in the moment. He shook T. J.'s hand and said "Sorry, buddy, I'm going to have to ask you to leave." He did.

I regained my composure. My mother stood behind Dad as if she needed protection. "What are you doing back there, Mom?" I asked. She stepped around him cradling a small buff-colored puppy, a Cocker Spaniel. It looked frightened and was squirming at being exposed. A neighbor had called Mom. "She's not the best dog, Karen. She was hit and kicked down the stairs, terribly abused by a grown man that needs a taste of his own medicine. She bites if you move too quickly, but I think she'll be fine with time and patience. I'm desperate to find her a good home." She'd called the right number.

Mom carried her to my room, set her on the bed, and left us alone. It was love at first sight. At least for me. She cowered as I

70

moved to pet her. "Ouch!" She nipped and drew blood, but just a little. I tried again. "It's okay, Blondie girl. You're going to be just fine. I wouldn't hurt you for anything." I understood her past and her pain. A while later, my mother came in the room. "Look at the two of you. She'll need your help to heal and to learn to trust again. And I think you'll need at least one new best friend in Ohio."

The move was still a month or so away when I saw an ad on television for permanent cosmetic makeup. I knew right away that I wanted eyebrows and eyeliner. PC Makeup would give me the color, definition, and expression I now painted on. I could wash my face without sending half of it down the drain. I could wake up each morning looking more like a woman than a blank slate. I felt joy and a new optimism. When I found a woman who did the procedure in Minneapolis I approached my mom about it. She slowed me down enough to get details including cost. I would ask them for a loan; one which I promised to repay in full. When Dad was sufficiently convinced, the appointment was made and we were on the road. In the car, my thoughts of "What if she makes a mistake? What if she pokes me in the eye and I lose my sight? What if I don't like the color? What if one brow is higher than the other?" All these things battled for position. But it was too late now. We arrived and I prepared myself as instructed. I was surprised how much each jab of the needle hurt and how the very first one brought back memories of Dr. Tibbetts. It took a long time. I endured, but not well. Near the end of the procedure, I started vomiting from a reaction to pain medication I had taken. This didn't help and slowed things down even more. Finally, it was over. I was shaking. The technician was shaking. Everybody in the room was shaking. Beauty had its price, beyond the $1,000 my parents paid. As intense as the pain had been, it didn't last. I had a "whole" new look. And I loved it.

The results pleased me so much that I decided to pursue the art, craft, and certification of micro pigment implantation myself. I breezed through local classes and bought the machine, the chair, and all the tools of the trade to take with me to Ohio.

My parents were supportive of my efforts and this made packing and moving much easier. I couldn't believe that I was actually going to move to Ohio, and alone. Well, with Blondie, and without my parents anyway. Unknown to me, my journey had already begun somewhere in my not-too-distant past. But I was aware of it now, aware that I was on a journey, a journey to Becoming. I was thrilled and fretful, a bundle of erratic thoughts. But I knew there was a reason God had placed this job in my path. The knowledge of that alone was sufficient.

I felt like some questions were going to be answered, and even though I felt very alone and anxious, I knew that I was moving forward, that I was on a path to a better life for myself. The break from my family, though difficult, was necessary. The rewards would justify the sacrifice. The decision was made. It came from some survival instinct aroused in me. My life would change. I knew that. And I felt I was ready.

Chapter Nine

Taking It All Back

I MOVED TO COLUMBUS, OHIO. I found an apartment, one with an office and allowed pets. I loved the feeling of independence again. It is difficult after being away at college, to come back home. My psyche was bruised. I grew into another person it seemed, and that person had become very cynical. Ohio, and the distance it put between me and my old life, would offer new possibilities. I was happy also to be away from T. J., yet lonely at the same time. My relationship with him left doubts in my head, the small fear that no one could really accept me as I truly was.

I worked as a counselor, with people who had no idea who I was. No one was aware of things I had been through the past few years, and the anonymity felt good to me. It gave me a way to begin, a certain hope that I could rethink things, maybe find out at last who I was, and try to deal effectively with the fallout of an abusive relationship.

Blondie made our home a sweet home. She came full circle from the shivering, snapping puppy in my mother's arms to a wriggling bundle of unconditional love and sloppy kisses. She softened me. She brought my guard down, tore my mask off and challenged my cynic.

When I felt proficient in my position at Great Expectations, I began advertising my permanent cosmetic abilities. In the trade called it *dermology*.[1] Dermology is not dermatology and there was some confusion at first, but slowly, I gained steady recognition as a competent dermologist. I helped a lot of people with alopecia and other problems. I was counseling, discussing things, things that many of us shared as bald women, common things that brought to each of us a sense of community, mutual understanding, and trust. We understood what it was like to get sunburned on our heads, to have it itch and peel and be miserable under our wigs. On the flip side, we were able to laugh about the time and money we saved in shaving creams and bikini waxes. Little did I know, that with every person I helped, it helped me in return. The exchange was mutual. What I gave brought returns. I learned that I really had a gift of empathy and could understand how others were feeling, before they even verbalized it.

I was giving back to them a feeling of "wholeness" and was beginning to feel differently myself. I began to live life outward

---

1 *Dermology is the application of permanent cosmetics. It is not considered a science or a field of medicine, as distinguished from dermatology. A dermologist is one who practices dermology.*

instead of inward. What I mean is, by helping others, by investing in the lives of confused, hurting people, I could no longer afford to withdraw into myself or allow my own hurt to remain master over me, my baldness, the whole image confusion I suffered. To be effective, I had to learn to give, and give, and give some more. And I learned that I could help others deal with a hairless way of life, because I was learning to do it myself. There was strength in numbers. The more people I shared my story with, more pieces of the puzzle began making themselves known to me. The prospect of finding a purpose in this world was overwhelming to me, wonderful. I was never certain, till now, what that purpose was, but I knew the revelation was close.

Sue, one of my clients, showed up at my office. It didn't take long to see she was scared. It took great courage for her just to come to me, or to anyone. I invited her in and realized that she too had Alopecia Universalis. We talked for a moment, enough to understand her shyness. I took off my wig and her chin dropped to the floor. I told her I had been bald for two years. Sue said she had lost all of her hair at thirteen. She was nineteen at the time of her visit. She had been hairless for six years. She had never met anyone with her condition.

At first, neither of us knew what to say, but once we began talking, we were good for hours. Two hairless girls. Two bald babes. The more we talked about our feelings and experiences, the better we both felt. Each little story, each anecdote revealed just how much the same we were. It also made the monster less and less threatening. It's so much easier to do battle with something when you know you're not alone. It relieved both of us of some hidden grief. It was beautiful. And I realized that every time I opened up to someone that was similar to me, I gained more acceptance of who I was. I realized I had a gift to help others feel better about themselves. Each permanent cosmetic makeup session turned into a counseling session for both me and the person in my chair.

Sue was thrilled with the results. There is no better feeling than to give back to someone the sense of dignity they felt they had lost or had been stolen from them. I knew this feeling too well, and to be able to give that "whole" feeling back to someone else was like a gift I could give myself. I enjoyed helping people so much, I felt badly asking for compensation. I often gave people discounts for this and that. I love helping others. It began to take on the strength of a vocation, a calling. And the more I help, the better I feel. I found myself being less cynical and more positive with each day.

I went out after work with my friends one night, and Al, the owner of the place I worked for, came with us. He was in town from Washington for a few days, helping us out. We were all having a friendly conversation, when I felt a pair of eyes on me. I looked up and Al was staring at me, with some boyish intent, I could tell. I was embarrassed and felt like a frightened school-girl, even though I was 23 years old. He gently took my hand from under the table. I smiled. Even so, I was still a bit anxious. My experiences with men had not been that good. I wasn't sure I was ready for another relationship. I felt uneasy, but decided to go with the flow and take my chances. I figured, "You only live once, and it's my turn to meet a nice man that will treat me well." Everyone else at the table was oblivious to all of this. It was like a game, and I thought that maybe I was ready to play again. I took my chances and continued with a great evening.

We continued on with our chit-chat for another hour or so, until it was time to leave. Al walked me to my car. He hugged me goodbye and tried to steal a "goodbye" kiss, but I quickly brushed him aside. I told him that I had a just ended a long relationship with this guy, and didn't feel that the timing was right. Al, ten years older than me and very sure of himself, leaned forward. He said, "I want to tell you a secret." I bent my ear to him and he said, "I think you are beautiful. I want to kiss you. I want to taste your lips!"

We looked into each others eyes, and my mind suddenly was a swarm of busyness. "Should I take a chance and let go of my past? Was this the end of my misery and the beginning of something wonderful?" So many thoughts filled my head, it was difficult to keep them tidy, well ordered. I smiled and nodded my head. His kiss was soft and sweet. I felt something stir in my stomach. My heart pounded out of my chest. I never felt so excited and happy all in one. The kiss seemed to last forever. I closed my eyes and enjoyed the moment. Al slowly pulled away and took my face in his hands. He told me how very special I was and how happy he was to meet me.

Before we went our separate ways, he invited me to dinner the next night, and I accepted. With another small kiss, I started my car and left. I felt as if I was floating. I felt so elated, and so nervous, too. When I got home, Blondie was waiting. I gathered her up in my arms and gave her a big hug and kiss. How easy it felt then to love. I took her out for a long and quiet walk under a starry sky. The smell of Al's cologne lingered on my cheek and mixed with the night air. It was, he was, elixir.

The ringing phone jarred the sweetness from the evening. I knew it would be T. J. so I did something I have never done before. I didn't answer it. There were a lot of confusing emotions tumbling about inside me. Why was I still concerned with T. J. at all? Why was I still tethered to him? And why was I excited about the prospect of something fresh and new, still warm on my lips?

All this was synonymous with my regaining control over my life, pulling the plug, burying the final remains of our relationship and the controlling factors over my life. I decided that I was through being the victim. It was finished. In one brief moment, in one clear flash of insight and maybe a little bravery, I made the decision that T. J. or no one else would run my life, that no one would torment me verbally, emotionally, physically, or any other way again. I felt that beautiful sense of hope again. This would mean victory over my fear as well, that I would become master over it. My insecurities had bound me to lies, to a vision of life that was distorted, founded on image alone, to guys who were all wrong for me, to false mirrors, and ultimately to a perception of myself that was destructive. This was the mountain I wished to reduce to rubble.

⌘⌘⌘

We drove back home, back to Wisconsin to visit my family for the weekend. My mom scarcely believed Blondie was the same dog I left with. Then she looked at me and said that I seemed different too. "What is it Honey? You seem happier or more rested?" She just couldn't put her finger on it.

"She's too thin, that's the problem." My Dad insisted. "Let's eat." They had prepared my favorite dinner, crab legs and asparagus. I sat in my usual place at the table and gave them the long and happy version of the people I had met, the new life I was making.

They responded by telling me they were proud of me and thought I was amazing and an inspiration to many. "Where did I get my strength from?" they wanted to know. Their words were kind and as necessary as they had always been. I chose to believe them. I was beginning to enjoy the thought of being myself, just me, just Jodi.

It was summer and they left for the cottage. I was packing my suitcase to go back to Ohio, when Blondie growled and tore out of the bedroom. A second later there was a loud banging at the front door. Through the peephole, I saw T. J. He knew I was there and was yelling and screaming, cursing me with every bad name he could remember. "Let me in Jodi, I am warning you! I will break that damned door down, you know I will!" He stopped pounding then and I saw the top of his head pass by a window. He'd find a way in.

I was so scared. I ran into the kitchen and hid from sight. I knew that he wasn't giving up and I would have a long night in front of me. He was back to the door, his fists beat harder and louder. It was the sound of our entire relationship—violence and demand, disregard and venom. I feared him and there was nothing about him that I respected any more. As I kept hiding, he got more and more demanding. I really thought that he would break the door down. *I'll huff and I'll puff and I'll blow your house down.*

I yelled back, "Go away or I will call the police! I don't want to see you again, ever. You need to leave!" That just angered him more and he started hitting the door over and over again, saying "You can't leave me, I won't let you! If I can't have you, no one can! Now let me in!" I heard a loud crack. His fist had broken through the hardwood door. Blondie went berserk.

"Ouch! You bitch! Look what you made me do! My hand is bleeding. Please Jodi, I need you. Please help me, it really hurts! Let me in. I will be good, I promise! Please, help me!" I was so fearful that he had taken things this far, but I knew he would hurt me if I opened the door.

"Go a-way! Go to the hospital if your hand is hurt that bad! I don't want to speak with you, leave!"

And at the top of his lungs, "I hate you, and I will kill you if you don't open this door, right now!" He began tearing the door apart and finding new combinations of words to hurl at me. Acid and vitriol. I ran into my parents' bedroom. Dad had a gun and I knew where he hid it. I took the weapon and ran back into the kitchen. Finally, I grabbed the phone and dialed 911.

"Please, help me! Please!" I pleaded with the operator.

I can't remember what I said to her, but her voice was soothing. "Take a deep breath Miss, don't worry, there is an officer in your area, I will have him there in just a few minutes! Stay with me, though, don't hang up, ok?" It seemed like hours, but within minutes the police arrived. I could see T.J. fuming as the police went through the routine of arrest.

"Bitch, I hate you!"

The three police officers put handcuffs on his wrists. The officer writing the report looked at me and understood everything. He told me I made the right decision, that I was brave, and now I was safe. "A lot of women will just take the abuse and never call for help. Good for you. You should be very proud of yourself!"

I gave a small acknowledgement while looking at the broken door and the commotion beyond.

They took him away, and that was the last time I saw T. J. I felt almost tranquil. Sure, I was afraid, but I wrestled it down, and the bad guy lost this time. Taking a stand, particularly against the confusion of emotion within me, had given me back some of the dignity and confidence that T. J. tried to take from me. I was in control again. I also made a pact that I would never let this happen to me again. I couldn't wait to get back to Ohio and flee this insanity. There was a sense of calm in my new apartment. There was peace. I was free!

Chapter Ten

Born Again

I HAD TAKEN THE FIRST STEPS to gain control over my life again, and it felt good. The abuse was behind me. I was still working as a counselor and a dermologist. I was helping people with alopecia, helping them to change their lives dramatically with permanent cosmetic makeup. With each person I helped, I was getting my life back. Each investment I made was bringing immediate returns to my sense of well-being.

The word got out that I was helping bald women, like myself, and that created quite a media stir. I began appearing on TV news programs and in the papers, telling my story, telling how I was able to help others like myself. I actually had to get a post office box for people to send me letters, because there was such a positive response. I still didn't realize my place in life, yet things were beginning to fall into place. Each person I helped allowed me to find more of who I was and to discover my purpose.

My mom was less than thrilled about me going public with my "condition." As I said before, in her eyes it was not right to let people know about your problems. She and I had a completely different opinion of confession. To me it was cleansing. For her it was overexposure. I know she has always meant well, that her motives were maternal and protective. But her perceptions of life and her applications were based on old judgments, old biases, perhaps handed down generation after generation. "What if someone sees that program in Wisconsin?" Meaning, "What if someone we know sees you bald and I have to explain things to them. This would be very difficult for me." Since she had never been a big "talker of feelings" this presented quite a challenge for her.

But I needed to do what I needed to do. I hired a modeling agency to help make sure I did this "coming out" most effectively. The Right Direction was the name of it. I had a complete portfolio taken of me with and without hair. I wanted to show people that being bald could be beautiful. I did a bit of modeling for them, and my confidence began to improve. I wanted to unravel all the tangles I had found myself in and being aggressive with it was the only way. All or nothing. I would take baldness to a level rarely ever seen. I would convince the world that BALD IS BEAUTIFUL.

My agent was a wonderful lady that said, "You look better to me without the hair, girl!" Rachel was a real inspiration for me and pointed me in the Right Direction (forgive the pun). She made me feel like I was a beautiful person within. She showed me how to tap into my inner beauty. I didn't know what this meant before, but I was quick to learn and it felt wonderfully liberating.

I made a new acquaintance, a young man named Mark. His mind, heart and soul felt evolved, I don't know how else to say it. I was attracted to him. He was kind and seemed to like me for who I was, with or without hair. I thought that this may the one, but even outside that consideration (that backfired on me before) he did something that was quite out of the ordinary, quite daring, actually. On my birthday, a day that came with unpleasant memories, he gave me a Bible.

"A Bible?" I thought. I was actually shocked to receive such a gift. Though I had become thankful on a few occasions and actually thought about God, it had been some time. Mark explained to me that he was a Christian. Earlier in my life, with Helen, I put up barriers, and refused to listen too closely. But now, after so many dramatic events, some of them dangerous, I was in a better posture to accept his testimony. I found myself listening intently, with a real curiosity, a curiosity that could have only been aroused in me by divine inspiration.

"God is hope to me, Jodi. I have been reborn in the spirit, and I have given all my control to God. I let Him handle my problems and I trust that he will guide me through tough times. All you need to do is believe and give charge of your life to Him!" In the past I would have nodded my head and gone on about my business, writing him off as another evangelical zealot. Not this time. He went on to explain, "You don't have to hold the weight of the world on your shoulders. You can simply offer yourself to God and He will prove himself faithful to take the burden on Himself. He gives strength. He gives new life. And most of all He is the god of hope, and makes it freely accessible."

The more my friend spoke, the more I considered deeply each word. All the stress, all the tangles, all the knots. I could let go of them? I could be released from their tyranny? I could be free, truly free? And happy?

Before my mind could fully comprehend, and before my mouth could form the right string of words, my heart offered up a prayer of forgiveness and I asked God into my life.

"God, I am a sinner! I have blamed you for all the bad things in my life. I blamed You for losing my hair. I blamed You for the abusive relationship. Forgive me for all that. Forgive me for all the things I can't even remember, things that I have done that are not pleasing to You. Instead of my trying to control my life, I ask You to direct me. Take this fear from me and show me the true path of life. I will follow. I submit myself, my complete self to You. I know You have a master plan for me. I'm willing to do what You ask of me. Give me empathy and understanding. I thank You and praise You for all You are in my life! Forgive me for not allowing You access to me, for being my own worst enemy. Take away all my control. Take away my pain, my anger, my sorrow, that I may follow the way of love. Give me a heart to trust in You, Lord!"

After nearly an hour of searching myself, of recalling my transgressions and pleading for their forgiveness, after begging for mercy and direction, and crying without shame or restraint, I surrendered all. I promised that this day my life would be changed. My clothing was soaked and I felt cleansed. I asked Mark for some time alone. Did he mind?

"Not at all." He understood completely. He took my hands in his and wished me great love and deep peace. Then he left and gradually disappeared altogether after a while—like an angel who had passed through my life and was on his way into someone else's.

I shed my tear-stained clothes and got in the shower. I felt as if a great weight had been lifted off my shoulders. My heart was light. I didn't understand much, and it didn't matter. My life was no longer my own. I looked into the mirror and actually saw myself as if for the first time. I saw a beautiful girl, and for once it was not just about image. It was not just about my looks. There was a new rule in my life. Vanity was deposed from its throne, from its dominion in my life. Sure, my convalescence would not happen overnight. But that didn't matter either. My perceptions would change. My mirrors would change. The world around me would change before my very eyes. Things that were once so critically important would be substituted for more substantial things, things that flow from the deeper springs of life. I would begin to understand what true beauty was, the kind of beauty that had nothing to do with the outward appearance, but the inward one, instead.

The heart would be sovereign at last. It would tell my mind how to judge, how to make assessments, the right assessments, based on truth that was eternal and immovable, a truth that was older than time. There was freedom in that kind of truth, just like Jesus said, "If you hold to my teaching, you are really my disciples. Then you will know the truth, and the truth will set you free."[1]

When you are able to accept yourself and love yourself, it can't help but express itself outwardly. You can offer real encouragement to others, without conditions. Perhaps God had brought me to Ohio for this very reason, to have me to Himself alone. I felt a completeness that I'm not sure I can describe. I actually began to feel comfortable alone, comfortable in my own presence, something I hadn't felt for a long time.

I started going to church and attending fellowships with Christians I could grow with spiritually. It was a happy time. I lost all control in church, and let myself cry. It was necessary, I suppose, to cleanse my heart of the debris. I fell in love with God. In doing so, I began to see all life differently around me. He truly gave me new eyes, that I might see clearly, and not only the beautiful things of life, but also the sorrowful. He gave me a heart capable of feeling large and life-giving things. He put words in my mouth for those who suffered, for those who crossed my path, that I might

---

1   John 8:31-32 NIV

comfort them and express His love. He renewed my mind, little by little, to what I was capable.

I am grateful that he saved me and that I was born again by the spirit! This gratitude would follow me for the rest of my life, into my workplace into my home, into my conversations, into my affinity for animals, and into those quiet thoughts when I consider who I am, when the question arises in my own mind.

There is life after hair loss. This became my motto. There is truly life after all illusions break down. Life after the fallout of our own misbelief. Life after all the pieces have shattered, after all the threads have come undone.

Chapter Eleven

Moves and Media

I TRULY BELIEVE I was removed from the abusive relationship with T.J. and directed to a place where I could be still and alone, free of negative input and influence. I was in Ohio to work, to have a life, and somewhere in the process I found God. I found myself as well, and the purpose that would give my life meaning. The mission was accomplished. I felt whole. I was ready to go back home and be a witness to my friends and family.

Since it was natural for me to share my journey with my family, Rick's greeting came as no surprise. And no great offense either. He called me a "Bible Banger." He grinned and rambled on how for Halloween, I should glue a pony tail to the back of my bald head, put on a saffron robe, and sell Bibles at the airport. Though his words had little of the effect they might have had in the past, I bristled nonetheless. I couldn't figure out if it was just an attempt at bad humor or if it was something else, some resentment hidden below the surface. In the end, I decided it didn't matter. I knew he wouldn't be the first, nor the only one to react to the "new" me. I actually laughed, and as I did, all opposing thought vaporized. Mom and Dad laughed with me. It was the kind of laughter that put us all at ease, and I settled into the comforts of being home.

The first thing on my back-to-Wisconsin agenda was to find an apartment where I could live and work, and then to find a church home. Becoming part of a new family of believers was important to me. I wanted to give my spiritual life every opportunity for growth and sustenance. My faith needed to be nourished and protected in the company of other believers, and I wanted to fit in, to find my place in the community of faith. Any non-denominational house of worship that taught the Bible, and believed Christ died on the cross for our sins, was fine with me.

Home, a place to work, a church, all of it seemed to fall into place as if by design. I was amazed, then questioned my amazement. Was it supposed to be this easy, this smooth? Of course, that was one of the promises, wasn't it? *Ask and it shall be given?*

The apartment I leased had an office well suited to my work. I planned to take my permanent cosmetic makeup corporation, Fabulous Faces, to new heights. I had never approached it as a full-time career before now. Already, voices rumbled inside me, and threatened to dampen my enthusiasm. "You'll never be able to support yourself. Get a real job," they said. "Be careful, be cautious." It sounded more like my mother than it did me. I had to separate my voice from hers. It took some doing, but I did just that. I followed the more hopeful voice within me, which I believed to be the voice of God, greater than all other voices, including my own.

A few clients came, then a few more. Many suffered different types of alopecia. Some were cancer survivors. There were those with motor or vision impairments who couldn't apply makeup, those with vitiligo who had lost their pigment. The numbers multiplied quickly, and mainly by word of mouth. I started making a good living. But more rewarding than the promise of financial independence, were the relationships that developed along the way. Not only did my clients leave looking better and feeling better about themselves, but I was able to share with them a story of hope. I was making a difference, one person at a time.

The physical closeness and the time required to design and deposit the tiny implants of pigment into the skin made conversation somewhat necessary. I'd inquire, in the cases of hair loss, what conditions brought it about. It was beneficial information. Often, embarrassment ran deep, as deep as my own. Privacy was important. Because I was a fellow sufferer, the trust came easily. You can't ask too much, too soon, but my office proved to be a safe and nurturing place. There was acceptance here, camaraderie, and true fellowship. My own story was received with hopefulness by every fragile new-comer struggling for far more than gracefully-arched brows. I believed each one left feeling less alone and more

BALD IS BEAUTIFUL—*My Journey to Becoming*

assured. I was performing a much needed service, and making new friends in the process. Their healing became my own. I felt a satisfaction that was deep and genuine. There was a place for me in this world, a place to serve and offer reassurance.

⌘⌘⌘

One night I went out to meet my youngest cousin, Debra. While waiting for her, I was approached by an attractive Asian-American man, curiously named Jose. He reminded me of Al, from Ohio, and that made him immediately comfortable to talk with. When I commented on the contrast of his Asian features and his Spanish name, he told me his father had studied in Spain and renamed himself Francisco. Jose had been named to honor his father's best friend. Jose himself spoke fluent Spanish, Mandarin, and perfect English. He was well dressed, and carried himself with a quiet confidence. He was born in New York and lived and worked there as an undercover agent for some undisclosed branch of Federal government.

Our courtship stretched over four short months. On month five, I took a leap of faith and accepted his proposal of marriage. We had become best friends. He also understood and encouraged my career. He swept me off my feet, and with as much charm as T. J. had, only without the psychotic behavior. I'll admit I was attracted

94

to the idea of living a glamorous life in New York, married to a man with such an impressive and exotic profession.

I had never been one to shrink from change, and therefore, with no real hesitation, embraced New York as my new home, my new "normal." The population and the energy of the city would prove to be a great source of opportunity to share with others not only what I did, but who I was. Being bald was still a novelty. In spite of the evolution of culture, and in spite of the presence in the media of personalities like Sinead O'Connor, change would be slow. It was an odd minority, an odd social demographic, one that easily hides itself. But the message that "Bald is Beautiful" was more than cosmetic. It was an attempt at wholeness for an individual, by whatever means we might discover together. I wanted to reach a lot of people. Instead of beginning again at ground level with Fabulous Faces, I started networking for spots on national talk shows.

Montel Williams invited me to appear with my sister-in-law on one of his shows. The topic was "Telling a Secret to Someone You Love." I remember it well, the whole first television experience. My stomach became uneasy. I spent a good deal of my preparation time in the bathroom. When it was time, I walked out on stage and told my story to Montel and his audience. My sister-in-law then joined me. I was to tell the story over again about the accident and when I came to the part about losing my hair, I was to remove my wig. I did just that, and when the hair came off, her mouth fell open. In her finest Bronx accent, she said something like "Get out of here, you didn't!" So I told her she was right, that I had just shaved my head to be on television, and of course, she didn't believe that either. She was hilarious. She made the show. The audience was in stitches. Then, leaning close to me, confidentially, she asked if Jose knew. I assured her that he did. When I followed with, " . . . and he loves me with or without hair," the world changed for me in an instant. The audience melted. It was a warm beautiful moment.

That first show did wonders for me. It paid me. It gave me an opportunity to come out about this aspect of myself in a very big way. It went against everything I was taught growing up about not revealing personal defects. The power of that show, and the largeness of my confession, gave me an added measure of self-acceptance. It didn't hurt either that Montel, hairless himself, told me I was more beautiful without hair than with it. I made bald look good that day.

Our performance, the tragicomedy it was, ignited a flame of interest that landed us on Talk Soup, over and over. I was featured on "Clip of the Week." The National Enquirer did a blurb using my professional head shot with my sister-in-law's reaction. I was a guest on the Jane Whitney Show, and a guest in the audience on the Ricky Lake Show. I was also to be on the Mike and Maty Show in Los Angeles, all expenses paid. I reveled in the limousines, the fine hotels, and the shops of Rodeo Drive like a kitten in cream. At Jose Eber's salon, I spent an entire afternoon trying on wigs while being filmed to the music of Pretty Woman. That was me, Pretty Woman. The salon transformed me into a "beautiful woman." I was in the green room, waiting to come out and tell my story again.

Unless I was naïve, I found it almost unbelievable that celebrities like Kenny Loggins and Judith Light would tell me that my life was an inspiration to them, that it was more interesting than their own. Or that Mike and Maty were genuinely moved to tears on the show. I was inundated with letters from people everywhere telling me how they could relate. So many people said "thanks" for sharing, for giving myself so freely to the world. Others said my bravery of coming out had helped them. It was the most liberating time of my life.

Chapter Twelve

Let There Be Light

MY INTEREST IN COUNSELING had an honest beginning. After graduating from college, I tried sales and just didn't have the belief it took to peddle something I had no personal investment in. It didn't last very long. It couldn't. I then took a job as a counselor at a weight loss clinic. I loved that. There was something about it, something very satisfying, and it seemed a closer fit with my own psyche. It was image based, after all. I was hired eventually by another company, another image industry company, Jenny Craig®. I had real aptitude for this—for image consulting. I had spent many years courting mirrors, hating them, struggling with them, pleading with them, despising them. Out of that time I acquired a certain knowledge that turned itself into a career.

Flight from a bad romance took me to Ohio and a job with Great Expectations®, a dating service. With each job, my pay and my position got better and better. My confidence rose as well, so I started spending more hours in my own company, Fabulous Faces. It's main concern was permanent cosmetic makeup application. This was my field. I had been groomed for it.

Everyone struggles at some time for identity. Charles Dickens called it "youth's struggle for life." That season when we fight through our illusions, through the storm of our misbelief, and, like Columbus, discover a whole new world on the other side. When we break free of the chrysalis, when we emerge with some truer (and adult) version of ourselves, an individual no longer supported by props and imaginary supports, but a whole individual with some real grasp of who they are.

My struggle for identity came earlier than most, perhaps. Some said as a child I was excessively talkative and hyperactive. That was a popular word then. I don't know. I'm not going to speculate. I just know that my mom used the word "willful," that I had to have my own way. It was a nice way of saying "whirlwind."

I was impatient. I had to win, if I competed at all. I had to be the best, the first. As I said earlier, "perfect" became an idol for me. I wanted to please, I lived for praise. I must not disappoint. I was walking at nine months. I was tying my own shoes at two years old. I bit my nails. I wiggled my feet and legs a lot. I had a nervous tick in my neck. And I had a dislike of being held. Funny, when I catalogue it like that, no wonder heaven had to intervene. Only a diety could straighten out a stew like that. And He did. Somehow He fit it all together. Not one small item on the above list could have been absent. He somehow saw order in it. After all, creation itself was a mess, wasn't it? I think one translation of the Bible uses the word "chaos." "Without form and void," the King James says. God saw something beautiful, and all He did was adjust the light. "Let there be light." That's what He did. And that's what He did for me, He adjusted the light. At just the right time in my own little history, He let me see what beauty there was beneath all this Jodi.

So what choice did I have? There was so much psychology in my brief tale, that it was in the direction my compass pointed me. I wanted to go back into Health Psychology. I wanted to work with the whole concept of image. My hair loss had long prepared me for this. I had years of experience with image and its torments, and, as I matured spiritually, its triumphs.

I applied to a number of schools and was accepted into an elite program at West Point Military Academy through Long Island University. LIU only allowed a small number of students to enter each year. They weighed professional experience, age, and grades. I wrote about being bald and wanting to help others. That helped me get selected.

For two years I attended classes at West Point with cadets, with officers, and a wide host of others. I loved the diversity. It was a good contrast to Wisconsin and Ohio. There was real regimen here. It was healthy for me at many levels. My favorite class was Therapy/Counseling in which we learned the fundamentals of becoming a therapist. Each of us worked with an upperclassman for the duration of the class. We also went through therapy ourselves twice a week. I learned more than I ever would have dreamed about my life and the complex dynamics of family and environment.

It was here that I sorted out all the pieces of myself and composed the above index of my Jodi behavior. This was the most eye-opening experience of my life. My pursuit of psychology, while my outward motive was to serve others, was as much for me. Through it I would mine my own depths, discover my own hieroglyphics, all my buried life, and make sense of it. This was at least my deeper intention, whether I was totally aware of it or not. I don't think I actually was aware of it, not at the time anyway.

It is difficult to change ourselves, much less others, but we can learn to change our reactions and our assessments of others and events that move us and our response to situations we cannot control. We can control ourselves, if we have the courage to learn to do so. We can choose to focus on the good things within us and know that the external doesn't really matter as much as we thought it did. I have made a life out of the outward expression, of applying makeup. But true beauty, the real kind, comes from within. I know that sounds cliché, but it happens to be true. I know. I was just hung up, like too many men and women, on the outward message. An image junkie, I thought little of and had no clue how to approach the inward realm. But once your perceptions become tame, once you come to reasonable, and hopefully, agreeable terms with the outward message, you can pursue true beauty, that to which only the soul has rights. My job is to help others come to terms with their appearance. It's a stumbling block for way too many of us, particularly today when *Image* is god and *Perception* rules. It's a difficult passage to undertake. It's Lewis and Clark all over again.

⌘⌘⌘

After two years, I graduated on the Dean's List with honors and a 4.0 average. I was proud and ready to "save the world." I still had no lack of ego. All new therapists make this error in judgment, I believe. The good ones admit it and work through it.

I interned with Dr. Henry Sobo, an internist practicing holistic medicine. He worked with weight-loss and weight-gain patients, those undergoing chemotherapy, and others with medical problems that could benefit from vitamins and supplements in addition to the other medications they were taking. I helped counsel them concerning their progress and fielded concerns about their new and enhanced supplemental diets. I focused on behavior modification techniques that made it easier for them to adhere to Dr. Sobo's advice and get the full benefits of the program prescribed to them. We were a great team. I loved working with his patients, and like them, was enlightened with new knowledge about the importance of purifying mind and body. All of this was near to my heart, and

I was certain that God had placed me here to help others and help myself.

I was infatuated with the process of learning and applied to Yeshiva University Fekauf School of Medicine in the Bronx, for my Ph.D. in Psychology. I enjoyed the program and, once again, found the broad cross section of people on campus to be unique and inspiring. I studied morning, noon, and night. Life as wife and student was good. I was busier than ever, but a new feeling rose up in me, a feeling that something was missing. We got a new puppy, a Rottweiler, who we named Morgan, but that wasn't it. The vacancy remained. I listened and I prayed. I let it circle about me and come close.

One evening as my husband and I talked together after dinner, the subject popped up with no warning. I stopped talking mid-sentence. When I began again, I told Jose that I had been having this odd feeling, like emptiness. Life was full in every way it could be full, but I felt an absence of something. Jose said he felt it too, and like me, wasn't sure what to call it or how to explain it away.

Chapter Thirteen

Jessica

WITH TIME IT CAME TO ME. A baby. My insides were warm for life. And now I knew that was it for sure. My husband smiled and agreed, telling me how I always knew exactly what he was thinking. He pronounced it a wonderful idea.

Early morning a few months later, I took a home pregnancy test. Jose was still asleep. As I waited in the bathroom for the results, I prayed, "Dear God, thank you for bringing my life together, and thank you for giving me the courage to be all you want me to be, daily. I give all my concerns to you, and ask that things go your way, dear Lord, according to your will." And then one final request, "Oh! And please let the test be positive!"

I felt emotional, honored to be alive and grateful for all I had been through. Ten minutes later I slipped the little stick from its cylinder. In its window was a bright and unmistakable plus sign. I was pregnant! I felt at ease and beyond exhilaration all at once. I was caught up in a miracle, one of the great secrets of life. The more gratitude we have for the blessings bestowed upon us, the more we open up our lives for even more happiness and wonder. Was this moment not living proof? I looked at the stick in my hand and went to tell Jose.

As I whispered the news in his unsuspecting ear, his reverie turned to revelry. He was ecstatic. He reached for me and we laughed and cried at the wonder of it. I called my mom and told her she was going to be a grandmother. We shared that moment of happiness together, even though we were hundreds of miles apart. She wasn't sure she was comfortable with the title of grandmother. It affects the vanity, and I suppose there was a strain of that in our camp. But together we had fun with the word. She was delighted. Of course, she asked me about the Ph. D., but that was to be expected. I continued with my classes, more eager to learn then ever. As the time passed, however, it became increasingly difficult to get in and out of the desks. My physical dimensions were changing, and the desk had no sympathy for me at all.

I enjoyed working out, and took pride in the fact that I was hardly showing. I took Blondie and Morgan running every day and did aerobics. I felt like a million bucks. I went to the doctor for check ups and Jose went with me. The doctor had told us that this was the visit during which he would put a fetal heart monitor on my belly to hear the baby's heartbeat. My husband held my hand as we listened to the most wonderful sound we had ever heard. A very rapid and swishy thump, thump, thump. There was life in me, other than my own, and I never felt so complete.

In addition to my studies, I read everything about pregnancy that I could get my hands on. I ate well, rested sufficiently, and kept exercising. I filled the house with uplifting music and thought good thoughts. I prayed for a healthy baby to fill our hearts and home. Indications were that it would be a boy.

The last trimester was here already and I was a picture of health. One afternoon I went outside for the mail. There was some construction on our street. I could smell the tar, it seemed dense. As I looked across the street at the beautiful flowers being delivered to my neighbor, I stepped on some loose gravel, lost my balance, and slipped forward. As I began to fall, I moved my leg in front of me somehow to absorb the fall, and landed on my knee cap and then my stomach. I lay there, afraid to move. I rolled over and sat up slowly. I felt a sharp pain in my belly and my leg was on fire. I had ripped my pants and there was blood. I struggled to my feet and slowly limped in the house, clutching both hands over my belly. I neglected my knee and immediately called my husband at work.

He hurried home. I called the doctor and told him what had happened. As doctors do, he gave me assurance that everything was fine, that such falls are not out of the ordinary. My husband took me to see him immediately. I sat back in the car and closed my eyes. The only thought running through my head was that the baby was safe. I held my husband's hand tightly. Neither of us uttered a word the rest of the trip there. Once there, I told the doctor what happened. He said, "First of all, you both need to take a big breath. God is very careful to put a lot of cushioning around the baby. You said you fell on your knee first, and by the looks of things, you really did some damage there, but probably not to the baby." He took the fetal monitor and placed it on my belly. "The baby is fine," he said. Hearing the heartbeat again put all other considerations to rest. Now I could go about the business of my aching knee. The x-ray showed I had fractured my knee cap. I was given a pair of crutches and a lecture about how careful I was going to need to be now.

Getting around was a challenge now, even the small tasks. Trips to the bathroom. Trips to the kitchen (which I was now making more than others). I started giving in to my cravings. I enjoyed being pregnant, and indulged every instinct. Hot fudge sundaes and big steak fries. Blondie was my partner in steak fries crime, she preferred them to running. I was not able to do much exercising and my weight gain became a bit too obvious. Blondie's too. There was little I could do but focus on getting better, and keep my mind occupied with happy prospects of baby and all.

It was difficult driving an hour back and forth from the Bronx a few times a week for classes, but I managed. I took my time and was really careful. Most people were very helpful when they saw this eight-month pregnant lady on crutches. Not something you see every day.

Mom and Dad flew in to New York the end of March to witness the birth of their first grandchild. It was now a few days past my due date and we all waited and waited, but no baby. My parents were doing their best to remain calm. They had just sold their home on Bologna Hill (so called because people had to eat bologna to afford the mortgage payments) and were waiting to hear about a counter offer they had made on their new home. While in New York, they received a call from their agent. Their offer had been accepted and they needed to get back to the closing within a few days. The anxiety mounted as we waited for the baby to drop into position, but no luck.

My dad had to catch a flight out the next day, and Mom was going to stay another three days, anticipating the arrival of the over-due one, but still no baby. Three days later my mom decided to change her ticket for another week, and then she would have to get back home to start moving into their new home.

One week passed. No baby. Finally, on April 9th 1996, two weeks overdue, the doctor decided to take the baby by C-section. I was very nervous as we made our way to the hospital. The tension was thick and very present around us. We arrived at the hospital and I was prepped for surgery. I took off my hair and put it over a box a tissues on the stand next to my bed. I could feel the baby kicking really hard, and its foot felt lodged up under my ribs. Soon a nurse was wheeling me down to surgery. While on our way, the catheter got stuck on the wheelchair wheel. What a mess I made. Urine was every where. The interruption was taken in stride with the nurse doing a few quick adjustments and ordering a clean-up. She comforted me with a laugh and assured me that I didn't need to worry about it. It happened all the time.

Surgery. I was sitting up and leaning forward as instructed when I felt a sharp poke and a burning sensation under my skin. They were giving me the anesthetic to numb my lower region. The numbness began and I was laid on my back. Two of my pediatricians entered the room. Soon one said "Okay, we just made our first incision, and we're going to spread apart your lower area, to reveal the baby." As they began using the spreader, I felt an excruciating pain. The doctors held a whispered conference and requested more anesthetic. I am highly sensitive to drugs, so they were very cautious and gave me a minimal amount. I was not fully numb. This was the most painful thing I had ever felt in my life. My husband was trying to get me to focus on his voice and my breathing when the new drugs took hold.

"We're almost there," a doctor said. "I see lots of black hair. If it's a boy, what are you going to name him?" I gave him a weak reply, "Jacob, we are going to name him Jacob." I looked at my husband, who nodded his agreement and watched anxiously. I couldn't believe what we were witnessing. The anticipation was wonderful. In a matter of minutes, the doctor held out our baby. "You've got yourselves a beautiful baby girl."

"A girl?" I asked. I laughed and cried. We hadn't been serious about wanting to know our child's sex before it arrived, but this little one now was a complete surprise. We'd name her Jessica Ann, all ten pounds one-half ounce of her. All twenty-one and a half inches. This was one moment in my life where the word "perfect" was the only one that applied. I was so drugged after the surgery, that my speech was slurred. I was feeling no pain when they wheeled me into a room with Mom and Jose along side. Soon they presented me with little Jessica, all clean and sweet, and bundled in a light nursery blanket. I undid the blanket and looked at her. She was plump and solid, beautiful, a real Pliszka. Her little eyes were Asian, like her father's. All the parts were there. Everything was working and in good order. I took her to my breast and instinct did the rest.

Soon after I recovered, my mom had to leave for the airport. She had changed her ticket three times, and this time she had to leave. I cried as she said goodbye.

They took the baby away for some tests during a shift change. After a reasonable time, I requested that a new young nurse bring Jessica to me. She went to the nursery and didn't return for over fifteen minutes. She came back, frantic. "I don't know where they put your baby. I am so sorry! Don't worry, I will find her!" After my impassioned plea, the nurse confessed, "She's not in the nursery.

There is only a little Asian baby with no name label." I looked at her and smiled. When she realized the comedy and the terror of it, her face turned bright red. She brought Jessica to me and placed her in my arms. It was over. My body would condense back to its pre-baby shape. Life was totally complete.

Chapter Fourteen

Change

MOTHERHOOD SUITED ME. I loved everything about it. Jose stayed home with me that first week after Mom left, but after that I was on my own. I got my books out, called Mom often and let the rest of mothering come naturally. It did, and Jessica was thriving, as new life should. As if giving birth wasn't miracle enough, knowing that her every need depended on me was the greatest, most moving and powerful feeling in the world. For the first time in my life I felt a true, compassionate, and complete love for another human being. The more I met and responded to her needs before my own, the deeper I loved her.

One evening when my husband came in from work I casually asked him to give his daughter a quick diaper change so I could finish dinner. His reply was "No!" and that I could do that. He had something else to do, other things. *"No problem. It's what I did now."* The diaper was changed and dinner was on the table.

"Is anything the matter?" I asked him. "You seem so quiet and preoccupied lately." I wondered if Jessica waking up during the night bothered him, or if I wasn't giving him enough attention. He took a long time to answer, then said he wasn't sure how to tell me this, that a great position had opened up in the field and he wanted to take it. I failed to see why such good news was difficult for him to deliver.

"That's great. I'm happy for you," I said thinking how proud I was of him for actively seeking a position that would better compensate him now that he had a child. No response.

Then finally he said, "It's in Albany, three hours from here."

I wasn't sure how to respond. Thoughts of packing and moving so soon after becoming a first-time mommy raced through me. But he suggested staying where we were, that he would work Monday through Friday, and come home on weekends. I resisted this suggestion more than the imagined difficulties of moving. Even though I took care of Jessica all by myself, I didn't like the thought of him being gone all week and just seeing us on the weekend. Though I wanted him to come to the conclusion himself and rethink this strategy, he remained firm, assuring me that I was strong and capable and he knew I could handle it.

"But who's going to take care of me?" I wanted to know. It hadn't been that long since the C-section, I was still stapled. I don't care how strong I was, I was new at all this. Our negotiation didn't last long, if you can call it that. I lost and submitted to my husband.

Before long I was sending him off at the first of the week with love notes in his pockets and the best blessing I could muster.

I called my mother and broke down. Instead of being sympathetic as I had hoped, she assured me, too, that I had been through situations more demanding than this, and not to worry. I could handle it. I thanked her for the encouragement then quickly changed the subject by bringing her up to date on her "already brilliant" granddaughter.

Weeks and months went by and it was still difficult adjusting to his absence. I missed his companionship and his coming through the door at the end of the day to join us as family. I wanted him home with us, involved in everyday milestones. Just the knowledge that he was near, had been comforting. I began to worry about his safety. His nightly calls got shorter, more monotone. They were more obligation than warmth. The frequency diminished too, from every night to every other night or less. We were slowly becoming strangers. My imagination worked overtime trying to speculate on his intentions, on his nights, on the company he was keeping. I looked for signs and clues on weekends but couldn't see any.

One particular weekend I reminded him of our upcoming fourth anniversary and suggested that we all take a trip to Wisconsin to the lake for a vacation. I wanted Jess to know the joy of the lake even as I had as a child. Jose didn't seem enthusiastic but with a shrug agreed to go anyway. A little later he said he thought we should fly, Jessica and me, because it was such a long drive from

New York to Wisconsin for a four-month old. He'd bring Blondie, Morgan and his dad with him in our new Nissan mini-van and meet us there. I didn't like the idea but I reserved a flight for Jess and me the next day. I wondered why I had restrained myself and not confronted him. I was ignoring and evading my own feeling, all the time thinking *"Who is this man and what has he done with my husband?"*

I planned and packed for the vacation, making long list after long list of what Jessica would need for her very first trip to Fish Lake. Jose packed for himself and I made another small list of dog things for him to bring by car. I couldn't wait. I was list happy and trip hopeful. Maybe the change would do us good. Maybe it would set our momentum in a more positive direction, westward— avoiding the south I began to feel in my heart. Thoughts of the cottage, the trees, wind and water made me homesick and happy.

It was departure day. We boarded and I strapped us securely into our seat, praying the cabin pressure wouldn't hurt Jessica's delicate eardrums. She slept all the way through her first plane ride.

The lake was everything I remembered, the sights, the sounds and smells. I was crushed with memories. That afternoon I sat in an Adirondack chair near the shore just as my mother had when I was young. She spent hours in that chair, sunbathing, reading and storm watching. She had a fascination with the wind and a nose for storms. When the winds picked up, some combination of changing light and subtle temperature caused her to snap her book shut and call for Rick and me, "Something's coming our way. Let's go!" That meant let's go to the end of the pier and watch it come. Across the lake, we watched the wind pummel the tops of the pines, then suck them back up and swirl them around for good measure. White-capped waves rushed and grew bigger, the dark clouds bore down on us but still we stood our ground. When the wind hit us, it whipped our clothes like sails and sent my long hair twirling like copter blades. Only when the clouds released their torrent was Mom convinced the storm meant business and sent us scurrying up the path to shelter.

From her carrier next to me, Jessica now watched the tall pines sway. She craned her neck to its fragile limits and took in all she was able. She added a soft cooing to the lake sounds. The water at the shore was warm and we sat in it together, Jess propped up between my legs. She seemed to love the place as much as I did. The fresh air wore away her energies and she slept nearly through the three nights we waited for her father. And waited.

On the fourth day they arrived. I dressed Jessica in one of her cutest outfits, the one most irresistible to her daddy. When I heard them drive up, I ran with her in my arms to welcome them. I held her forearm up, waving her pudgy hand hello.

It was a great week at the cottage, Fish Lake magic. The four of us, with Blondie, Morgan and our luggage in the rear, drove south to visit with my parents for a few days at their new home.

They called it a gentlemen's farm. I hadn't seen it yet. There was a contemporary house and a barn on four fenced acres. A small menagerie consisted of two horses, two dogs, four barn cats and five miniature donkeys. Even at four months, Jessica was transfixed at the sight of them. It was wonderful here, being near Mom and Dad again, watching them be grandparents. Suddenly, I was melancholy but couldn't exactly say why.

The vacation ended all too quickly. Jose, his dad and the dogs left early, early enough to make a leisurely drive out of it and get settled in enough to pick us up at the airport. Jess and I stayed on. My husband and I agreed to talk every night on the phone as they made progress on the road toward their destination. Talk was small.

They arrived on the third day, and I expected him to call before he went to bed. But he didn't. I rang our number in New York. No answer. Nothing. I persisted. We were flying home the next day and I wanted to be sure everything was in order. Finally, very late that night, my parents' phone rang and I jumped out of bed for it.

He began slowly and told me to sit down. I could hardly hear him. He couldn't call me before, he said, he needed more time to think. People told him that he should get out now. Leave before the baby got old enough to know what was going on. Leave so there would be no trauma of leaving. What did he mean "getting out?"

117

Out of our marriage, away from Jess and me? Who was telling him these things? I didn't want to hear any of this.

"Look, this is just not working out for me."

"What do you mean?" I reminded him that we just celebrated our anniversary. We were together and everything seemed okay. Why hadn't he talked with me in person at the lake? There were plenty of chances. No response again. I waited for him to talk and when he didn't, I exploded. What kind of a coward would end a marriage and leave his child on the phone? More silence.

He gave me instructions instead of answers. To tell Jess he loved her. He would be gone, moved out, when we arrived that next day. He apologized one more time and that was all. I went off again, without muzzle or bridle, crying out at random whatever came into my head. I pleaded about getting help. I asked for answers. I demanded answers. But he had hung up and it was all over.

My parents came out of their bedroom. They took the phone from me and wanted to go back to bed, reserving the right to talk it over in the morning. But I couldn't wait. Not for this.

"He's leaving me and Jess!" I shouted and cried. I tore at the buttons on my pajamas. The more I thought about it, the more I cried, and the more I cried, the more out of control I became. I started hyperventilating. There was compression in my chest and I wondered if I was having a heart attack.

My mother tried calming me. She talked softly. She took my hands and again reminded me that I'd been through worse situations than this. I couldn't remember one and challenged her to refresh my memory. She brushed me off telling me to draw on my strength from the past and not to let this ruin or control me. She told me I had the control. *"You have the control. It's in you. Do you understand that?"* Between sobs and gulps of air, I nodded in her direction. Quieting, I heard every word she said, and while I don't know how because my grief was overwhelming, I internalized her words, and turned them to belief somehow inside me. This time I knew I wasn't alone. I had a beautiful daughter and a promise that would not be broken. *I will never leave you or forsake you.*

My eyes were red and puffy in the morning. But something had happened to me in the night. My dad sat on the bed and watched me pack. I told him not to worry. Everything would be fine. He had raised no quitter.

Our goodbyes at the airport were harder. After all the advice and comforting things said in the car, it was my mother I remember most in the last moments together. She put her hands on my shoulders and faced me squarely. She knew it would be a difficult journey, but said they were both there for me, and for Jess. They would be there for us, always. Again, belief quickened in me.

⌘⌘⌘

My hand trembled as I put the key in the door. It was more than just a door opening; it was meeting the unknown, the mystery of the unpredictable. I asked for strength to meet the challenge. Blondie and Morgan greeted us, happy and wagging and trusting as usual. Though there was nothing usual about the moment, seeing them thrilled me, and made looking around at everything else less shocking than I had feared. I unpacked and we settled in.

The weight of nurturing and maintaining calm and sensibility in this place we knew as home fell upon me. I understood the urgency of their dependence, the three of them. I was certain that this baby could pick up things and I wanted to protect her from fear, from the mess that had been made of things. I would do whatever it took to protect my child's soul from the infection of a failed marriage. I took time to prepare myself, to make every exchange with her count. We both needed reassurance.

The answering machine blinked. There was one message. I pressed the button thinking it was probably my parents wanting to know we arrived, or possibly Jose had thought better of things and had left word for us. It was a woman's voice, angry, mocking. Not addressing me, she called someone in the background a loser, a sorry pathetic loser. Sleeping with her and making promises he didn't keep. I hadn't thought about an affair. We had talked about it, each assuring the other of the impossibility of it. Of course, I burdened myself with questions why. Had I gained too much weight with the pregnancy? Had I lost my bubble and fizz as a wife?

120

Part of me prayed for the marriage to be saved. I'd do whatever I needed to be a good and faithful wife. I remembered my own words, *"I give all my concerns to you, and ask that things go your way, dear Lord, according to your will."*

But it wasn't to be. The divorce was bitter. The finances were shambles. We lost everything. The house I had put my life savings into and borrowed for from my parents was lost in foreclosure. He filed Chapter 13 and dragged me down with him. Everything was gone.

I assumed that the divorce struggle and nights of sobbing had something to do with the new hoarseness in my voice. When it didn't get better, I consulted a physician and learned the polyps had returned. They'd need to come out. Mom came for the surgery and recovery period. I couldn't talk for two weeks, but somewhere in the vocabulary of a two-year old, Jessica found the perfect way to interpret my wishes to my mother.

My child remained oblivious to the changes going on around us. She was all play and fairytales. She loved putting my wigs on her head or insisting that Blondie or Morgan play the part of goldilocks. I kept the camera loaded and ready. Her innocence, her love, her acceptance of me bald or hairy kept me focused on the things in life that are true, and good.

Before we were evicted from the house, I came downstairs late one night to do laundry. Blondie was lying in the middle of the floor wheezing and coughing. Her lungs gave off a crackling sound and blood trickled from her mouth. I gathered Jess and rushed Blondie to the vet. She was in congestive heart failure and she died there, behind a wall that spared us from the sight of it. I made arrangements for her body and left clutching Jess in one arm and Blondie's favorite blanket in the other. The pain was wretched, the consolation sweet, *"All dogs go to heaven."*

When Jose surfaced again, he'd grown a mustache and got himself a tattoo. He was smoking, drinking, and riding a motorcycle. Most difficult for me was that he openly dated. He married and moved to Peru when the divorce was final.

The divorce process dragged on for two years. But Jess and I went on with our lives. We grew closer than I would have imagined possible. I left my doctorate by the wayside. Being Mommy was the best title I would ever hold, I knew that. I began seeing a Christian therapist right away and worked part time as a therapist at a psychotherapy center where I could bring Jess and her sitter while I saw patients. We met a lot of angels in disguise.

One in particular we shared a home with. Michael was our rock, a wonderful Christian friend that opened his arms to us. He loved and accepted both of us and became our closest friend. Through it all I suspected he wanted more from me than I was prepared to give to a friend. Although the comfort of a deeper more intimate and loving relationship was tempting, I couldn't. I was numb and not even divorced yet. The thought of rebounding with anyone, even this saint of a man, was inconceivable. He understood.

God kept us in His care and healed us a little each day. So did my parents. They called often and flew to New York to see us, sometimes bringing Grandma Marge along. When Grandma held Jessica and talked to her like the little person she was, I was overcome with emotion witnessing the beauty and the blessing of our four generations of women. Memories of Grandma rushed me. She had taught me to walk and to tie my shoes. She had cared for us one year Mom and Dad had gone to Spain. When they returned Rick and I looked like chipmunks—we had the mumps. Grandma took it all in stride. She was our private Disneyland. Later, she visited her own daughter when I got older. Mom would do her hair up in the old-fashioned rollers just like she liked it. Grandma was gentle, she loved all living things. I loved her kindness; how she never ever said a bad word about anyone. You were safe with her, assured she saw you in your best light. I could see the things I had treasured about her all along but couldn't fully understand or give voice to until I became a mother myself. Things weren't always easy for her with Grandpa, but nonetheless, she baked him fresh bread every day and honored him all the days of his life. The memory of her sweet rolls still made me salivate. I couldn't tell now if her sense of perception was getting weaker or her resolve to be agreeable was getting stronger, but she often commented on my hairdos and how much she liked them. I once tried to tell her that I had lost my hair but to this day, I can't tell you if she knew or not.

One afternoon, Jess and I were watching the Animal Planet and we both fell in love with a hairless, Sphynx cat. I'd never seen one before and I laughed out loud thinking *"God has a sense of humor. This has to be my soul pet!"* Jess was two at the time, but I thought since her mommy was bald she should have a bald pet as well. She was used to seeing me around the house, bald and without eyelashes, or wearing a bandana if it was cold. She'd rub or grab my head and sometimes pluck at the curiosity of her own hair. The 'soul pet' humor was therapeutic. I found a local breeder and brought home this little pink cat with big ears and skin that felt like hot suede. He looked so much like the Gremlins character, Gizmo, that's what we named it. Jess would understand that it is fine for people and even pets to look and be different. She would learn at an early age that it was what was on the inside of a person that mattered most.

The two of them immediately began the business of growing up together. Jess was into coloring. She loved washable magic markers, and liked to draw pictures with them on my bald head. It was our special secret, her artwork under my wig whenever we went out.

Our bond grew stronger each day. I was grateful for such a beautiful gift. Mine was a sacred task, that of guidance, of leading my daughter in a path of wholeness, of balance, of tolerance, and living outside prejudice.

Part of her development would hopefully include having a faithful father figure. Jose had not seen her in over a year and a half, and it seemed obvious that he wasn't going to. Michael had served as a steady and wonderful stand-in but in fairness to him, it was time for us to move on and let him find the love he deserved, and wanted. I wondered if I could ever find this kind of love, gentle, and unconditional, from any man.

There was one certainty. My father, Jessica's grandfather, was a rock. He was the only male part of our life that was solid. He welcomed us with a complete embrace, outside mere obligation and duty, but with genuine love. Within a month, mother and daughter were packed. In Wisconsin life could begin all over for us. There were happier roads ahead.

Chapter Fifteen

Coming Back Home

COMING BACK HOME was the right decision. It put distance between me and a shipwrecked marriage. It also placed me and my child in a sanctuary, in the warm safe reaches of my family. The change was filled with promise. And, I was different. The long painful divorce, and the early years of parenthood had seasoned me. My mother liked to say that I had lived the life of a sixty year old by the time I was thirty. All the disappointment and bitterness of my former life with Jose were memories behind me now. The sharp bitter edges had worn smooth. Once free, I even found myself rejoicing. We were better off without him. Life could mean something altogether different now, and held much greater expectations. No wonder I felt vibrant, with the energy of a teenager. I had a zest for life and was determined to keep a cheerful countenance, to remain a "child" at heart no matter what the journey asked of me.

Fortunately, my father owned a number of rental homes, the largest and finest of which had just been vacated. Jess and I moved in. She was four already and I planned to stay long enough to free myself from Jose's debts placed in my care. After that, I would find a home for Jess and me, one that we could call our own. There was plenty of room and light in our new place. We loved it. Gizmo and Morgan, like us, survived a case of the jitters on the move from New York and were adjusting well.

Our homecoming could not have happened at a better time as it concerned Grandma. She had been deteriorating and was now in a nursing home. The roles of parent and child reversed. Jess and I visited her and often drove her to Mom's where the rituals of bread baking and hair rolling continued. I wanted Jess to spend as much time with her as possible. Time was limited, however. Alzheimer's stole her memory and her speaking ability, osteoarthritis her motor skills. One afternoon when we were alone in her room, I told her she was very brave for holding on. Then I assured her, as Mom already had, if she needed to go we understood. "Don't worry, everything will be okay." I held her hand and let my tears fall. I wasn't sure she was listening or if she heard me at all. Then she squeezed my hand and whispered, "I love you." I brought my face close to hers and said I loved her too. I called her Grandma for the last time. She died that evening. Mom and I went as soon as she got the call. Grandma's body was there but "she" wasn't. Her soul had vacated. Perhaps it hovered above us now in the room. I wasn't sure but in this moment, I reconfirmed my thoughts of heaven, and was sure she was on her way. I thanked her for touching my life, and the lives of so many, in a way that only she could. I'd carry her memory with me. Her strength would be my shield for what would come. She would be my guardian angel until we met again.

It wasn't long before I reacquainted myself with some of my old friends. One of them, Vickie Bowe introduced me to the idea of triathlons just at the time when I was looking for something extra to do. Triathlons were held all over the country. They included swimming, biking, and running various distances. I allowed myself one small moment of fear about being hairless under my swim cap and helmet, then thought again. Hair was heavy, hair was weight, and every ounce of it would slow me down. Who needed it? I'd wear a bandana to protect my head from sunburn.

The combination of sports was physically challenging, and if there was a competitor inside you at all, large or small, these events had their way of bringing them out. It appealed to me at that level. I hadn't indulged the competitive side of me in years. Vickie was really excited about them, and her energies were contagious. She met so many people, had gone so many places, and she'd never looked so fit or healthy in all the years I had known her. I decided to give a try.

We got a family membership at the YMCA so I could train, and Jessica could have fun, as well as be close by. In good weather and bad, she was a part of my training. Swimming was our favorite sport and we were in the pool almost daily. When it came to biking, I pulled her behind me in the "alley cat." My quadriceps developed like steel springs. The resistance caused by Jess being attached, actually helped my training. I was stronger because of her, and cycled like the wind when she was unhitched.

I joined the Tri-Wisconsin Triathlon team and started competing. Competing was still a part of who I was. It brought back memories of my youth. I had to win. It was like a fever in me back then. The stress I imposed on myself, while I can't be positive, may have been sufficient enough to induce the first bald spots. With so many years between me and those girlhood days, the competition I faced now was mainly with me, myself. Did I still have the right stuff? The drive and kick? Could I run a little faster this time? I looked to the stopwatch on my Timex for the answer. Yes, I could. Could I pull out another five laps of smooth, clean strokes? Could my legs pull me up just one more hill? Now I competed for the sheer joy of it.

After one year on the Tri-Wisconsin team, I took first place in a short triathlon, aptly called a "Tiny Tri." I competed in a number of local triathlons and one weekend went to Madison for a bike race around the capital. I took first place in my age division. I had natural strength and ability. I was also having fun. Triathlons build character. They keep body, mind, and spirit healthy. Not only that, but I found myself in the midst a whole new community of friends.

Still, in spite of the joy of newfound friendships, my favorite part of these events was approaching the finish line with lactic acid screaming in my legs and my eyes scanning the crowd for Jess and my parents. The combination of intense physical stress and the exhilaration of spotting them as I crossed the finish line was enough to make me weep.

Back home, Gizmo and Jess were always together. They played every waking hour but I wondered if Gizmo might be longing for a pal like himself. I saw an ad in the paper concerning a Sphynx breeder in town, Scheherazadectz Sphynx. There was a new litter ready for sale.

I felt an instant connection with the breeder, Kristen. Like me, her love of animals ran deep. It was visible as she moved carefully among them, picking each one up and holding it out to us in introduction like a favored child. I remember liking this very much about her, it endeared her to me. After we had seen them all, I was about to sit on the couch when Kristen cried "Wait!" I jumped up and followed her eyes to a blanket I was about to sit on. Hiding it were two of the tiniest wrinkled kittens I had ever seen. One was so small it fit easily in the cupped part of my hand. It was the runt of the litter, the "underdog." It was also our choice. Isabella went home with us that afternoon.

Jess cradled her on our trip back, bringing her close to her face for inspection and telling her all about Gizmo. What would he think? When we opened the door, he was sitting there, waiting.

Now whether this was by accident or he was equipped with some special knowing, we weren't sure, but we presented him with his new friend, and the rest is history. They were made for each other, the perfect pair, happy and hairless as they were.

We took them everywhere, Morgan too. Bella often road in the cleavage of my sports bra and drew a good deal of attention. The five of us drove to the cottage for a week's vacation.

I had not been up north in a very long time, not since Jose. The time before that I suffocated under a wig, too afraid to wear it in the water and too afraid not to. I was certain in that visit that the carefree days of my childhood there were gone forever. Still I loved it, and now there was Jessica. She deserved a rich childhood of her own.

I relaxed my grip on vanity enough to stop wearing false eyelashes, and I wore hats and bandanas on my head. The first time I saw Uncle Jim and some of the people at the lake I knew as a child, no one said anything derogatory about my changed appearance. I breathed a sigh of relief and proudly introduced Jessica and our little four-legged family.

It was hot and Jess was drawn to the water. I took my hat off, put her in her life vest and floaty and walked down the grassy path to the beach. When my toes touched the water, I let out a shiver. It was refreshing and cool; precisely how it felt to be here once again. I waded with her, deeper and deeper. She was all squeals and laughter, "Mommy, let's swim!" There was magic in those words!

131

They unleashed the porpoise in me and I dove in. The chilly water hit my bare head and rushed over it. It felt like heaven. Strong from triathlon training, I pulled Jess all over the lake. For nearly three hours, the two of us played in the water, both of us children.

One morning Jess and I were at the kitchen table drawing pictures for each other. She drew a very fine picture of Bella and asked me to draw a picture of Gizmo. As he sat there on the table pawing at Jessica's moving crayon, I watched him. I mused on his uniqueness, memorizing his odd angles, and set my crayons to work. The drawing surprised and pleased both of us. Gizmo's beauty and likeness had been captured. Even he seemed startled seeing his image looking up at him from the page.

I can't imagine what it was in that moment that triggered such a question, but Jess asked my why her eyes were a different shape than mine. As I scrambled for a way to help her understand her father's Asian-American genetics, she asked another question, as unexpected as the first. "And how come you don't have any hair, and I do?"

I smiled and set my crayons down, thinking quickly. I scrambled. I mean I knew the time would come someday for us to talk about it, but I wasn't totally prepared for it to come so soon, and I wasn't sure I had the just the right language to make any of it clear. I assured her that her questions were good ones. Then, at that very moment, Gizmo sprang off the end of the table and landed head first in my lap. Was he trying to tell me something? Jess said, "Silly kitty!"

Gizmo sat there like he was waiting for the story to begin. And so I began by telling Jess the story of Gizmo and how he was different from other kitties because he didn't have hair either. I didn't want to be too long, but as I talked, the idea of actually writing her a story materialized. I'd write a children's book using the kitties as stars. My words would become their thoughts. Kids relate well to animals and stories. It seemed to be a very good way for me to share a lesson about being different. Since Jess and I had just been drawing pictures, I suggested we write a book about Bella and Gizmo and how they might feel different because they had no hair. She loved the idea. And that is how "Bella and Gizmo's Adventures" began.

We finished the week out at the cottage by writing the book. One wasn't enough it seemed, so we wrote a second and called it, "Bella Gets a New Sweater." That's how it went at the lake. It was always fun and relaxing, and every now and then, productive.

When we got home I took the books and a handful of photos and drawings to the *Look Good, Feel Better* meeting later that week. This (now international) organization began in 1989 with one person, a woman who was so depressed and self-conscious about her appearance after undergoing cancer treatments, she wouldn't come out of her room. In my area, there were plenty of singles, wives, and mothers experiencing the same issues. I read our stories to their children and showed them the pictures. Seeing cats without hair captivated them. By the time the stories were over, they were fascinated with their new heroes Bella and Gizmo, and were no longer just curious, but I believed more accepting of all creatures without hair. It was a subtle lesson in tolerance, a way of perceiving the world and the creatures who inhabit it, creatures like ourselves and those who are different than us. Several parents encouraged me to get the books published. I thought it was a great idea. And I was off to find a publisher.

Chapter Sixteen

A New Door, a Publisher and a Stuffed Cat

I SEARCHED THE INTERNET FOR WEEKS, targeting publishers most likely to have an interest in the two children's books. I prepared each submission in proper format, and sent them off with prayer and a lot of raw belief. Within weeks, the first reply arrived in a return envelope I had stamped and addressed (SASE). The rejections soon added up, but my determination never wavered. Letter after letter came. Every time I went to the mailbox I went through the same ritual. I prayed. I crossed my fingers. And I closed my eyes. I didn't let myself get discouraged. At the close of almost every letter was a personal note of encouragement, simply saying "Don't give up, great project, just not for us." Things like that. Some publishers actually gave me advice about where I might take the book. After nine months of rejections, I began to rethink things. I began to think about my next approach.

Meanwhile, Jess was growing up fast. She was in school and loving it, doing well. We also enjoyed the YMCA together almost every day. The Y offered Songahm Tae Kwon Do classes for children and I asked Jess if she was interested. She was. I watched her in her first class through a large window. She looked cute in her sweats. By the next class, she was in her dobok, the traditional crisp white uniform fashioned for unrestricted movement. She wore the white belt of a novice. Before long she graduated to the orange belt, then yellow, camouflage, green, and purple. She progressed eventually to the blue belt, and was gaining excellent control of her movements. I helped her as much as I could with her daily form and now she reeled me in. I enrolled.

I wore a wig during class thinking of Jess and not wanting to call attention to myself. I thought it would be fine at first. Of course I put my whole athletic self into the class, not to mention the old drive to achieve. But the intensity of fast spinning and the high kicking so characteristic of this martial art, made me sweat. It ran down the back of my neck, between my breasts, and into my eyes. The perspiration stung badly, and though I did my best to wipe my eyes, there were times I would forget that my permanent cosmetic makeup had faded, the epidermal issue had given way, and my eyebrows were only painted on. They often came to rest on the back of my hand in a dark brown smudge. I interrupting the flow of class to visit the restroom and apply and reapply eyebrows and eyeliner. At the end of an hour, my wig was always saturated. This meant more frequent washings, which shortened the life of the wig. It also meant a whole new set of comfort and health problems during the winter. I had to do something.

Attempting a solution, I placed a few Bounty paper towels under my wig. This worked until a fellow student asked "Ms. P, what's that on your face, tissue?" Jess told me there was a paper towel hanging out of my wig. I ran out to make repairs. I was embarrassed. I wasn't sure what Jess felt. Her sense of self awareness wasn't as advanced or wounded as mine. But now what?

The answer appeared the next day in a magazine. I read that men and women in the military used panty liners under their helmets to stop the sweat from rolling into their eyes. I had to try it. If it worked for them, it might just work for me. I used three of them to line my wig cap. It felt soft and cushiony. They were even lightly scented, and the hotter I got the better they smelled. And though they worked quite effectively, I began to feel the idea to be a bit undignified. Didn't our military deserve better than wearing feminine hygiene products on their head? And surely there were others out there like me. Who else wore helmets, caps and wigs and were having a similar problem? What about fire fighters, cyclists, construction workers? A whole world within a world had sweat running in its eyes.

I returned to the web and began to search for products that could be used under wigs, hats, and helmets. I found nothing. Nothing. And I couldn't stop thinking about it. I was at the edge of some discovery. I knew it. I researched absorbency and wicking materials. What elements could be put together to take care of oil and perspiration? What was the ideal shape? How could materials be assembled or bonded together? I studied chemical, thermal, and mechanical bonding processes. I studied lightness, coarseness, and skin sensitivities. I studied the design and construction of wigs with different types of caps and hair. My mind was racing, but not out of control. There was focus. My thoughts and ideas had momentum and a direction. Maybe this is what inspiration felt like.

The decision to invent the product myself followed naturally. It seemed to present itself to me after all. I phoned my parents and told them about it and warned them that I might need some financial backing. What did they think? I gathered Jess and my ideas and headed to their house to discuss it further. My mother is an accomplished equestrian and has been for years. She showed me an article in her "Dressage" magazine, and in one section I read, "The back of my horse trailer looked like a feminine hygiene accident, with all the strips from panty liners lying on the floor". This horseman too, had used them under his dressage helmet. This is precisely what I was talking about. How many more signs did I need?

Back on the internet, I Googled "invention help" and the door to the world of invention appeared before me. I called the number, made an appointment, and took my dad along to meet Gary Jensen at InventHelp^{SM}. He soft-sold us on the merits of his company and gave us a helpful overview of the inventing process. We left well informed and promised to get back to him. My excitement was mixed with relief, with a stronger sense of hope, and a feeling of accomplishment. InventHelp^{SM} represented themselves as America's leading inventor service company. Their purpose was to attempt to submit their client's invention ideas to industry. We researched other organizations but returned to InventHelp^{SM} with confidence. An enormous amount of paperwork was required— brochures, a patent application, and other legal documents. We completed them all and called my product "Headline IT!" All we had to do now was wait. Pray, keep my fingers crossed, close my eyes, and wait.

While waiting, I returned to the business of finding a publisher for the children's books. It had been nearly a year since the last rejection letter. I was led to Nightengale Media LLC, and its founder, Valerie Connelly. She read my submission and responded within twenty-four hours. She understood my vision, the great benefit my hairless cats could bring to a child's world. I met with her, and she seemed sincere, as well as genuine. And she was in Wisconsin, like me. We signed a contract and the books began their little journey to publication. She and her husband, Mike, are wonderful to work with. I now call them friends, and feel that they are my partners as well, dedicated to helping me fulfill my mission. Mike is a talented Webmaster. He designed and built my web site.

Just before the books were published, it became obvious that Morgan was losing her battle against an aggressive cancer in her mouth. It had appeared quickly, now there was nothing else to do to slow its march and stop its victory over her. I prayed that releasing her from her suffering was the right thing to do. Gone was our Morgan. She'd been a surrogate indoor pony for Jess and the giver of exquisite tongue baths to Gizmo. We all loved her and would miss her.

As soon as the book was published, I began to promote it. Barnes and Noble®, at Mayfair Mall, was the site of my first two book signings. I met many outstanding children and their families, some of whom were facing hair loss issues themselves. I prayed that the combination of my presence, my positive attitude, and the books themselves would be a source of hope and inspiration for them.

I wanted to have stuffed animals made to look like Bella and Gizmo. Stuffed animals had always brought me joy and comfort as a child, as they had for Jess. For this reason, I thought they would be a fine accompaniment to the books, and an additional comfort to children with or without hair.

I went back to the internet and searched for toy companies who might be interested in this. I started with eight companies, and narrowed the search one at a time. As the prototype phase neared, one company, Sunindo, stood out above the rest. They were instrumental in helping choose color, fabric, and texture.

They made a prototype of Bella first. Within a few months, six hundred little Bella dolls were in our basement, ready for sale. My plan was to let the sales of Bella generate enough capital to do the same for Gizmo.

Bella and the books were a hit. I submitted them for the Parent to Parent Adding Wisdom Award, the only award of its kind recognized by Disney. As I had hoped, we won *Best Children's Book of the Year* and *Best Book and Doll*.

Life was turning favorably in our direction. I suppose my little rituals paid off; plus hard work, perseverance, and tons of belief. And even as we were caught up in this unbelievably wonderful turn of events, the patent arrived in the mail.

Chapter Seventeen

Reality TV or Fantasy World

IN LATE NOVEMBER I received a postcard in the mail that said ABC's American Inventor auditions. I thought this was another hoax or a gimmick. I discarded the postcard and forgot about it. Jess and I went to my parents' house.

She ran into the kitchen and said, "Mommy, you have to come here, Grandma has to show you something!" I followed Jess and she handed me a newspaper. To my amazement, there was a huge ad that read "ABC's American Inventor Auditions."

"See Mommy? This is real!"

American Inventor was legitimate. It was another reality show from the makers of American Idol that was created by Peter Jones (one of the show's judges) who after approaching Simon Cowell, brought it to the US. I was just curious how they got my name. My mom suggested that the show probably did a patent search and my name came up. The question that came up next was, "Why not?"

The day before the audition, my mom called me to say Jess could sleep overnight, so I wouldn't have to wake her in the morning, and Dad would go with me, if I decided to go. I decided to go through with it. The audition was being held in Chicago at Navy Pier. It was first come, first served and the doors opened at 8:00 a.m. I gathered up my patent and the brochures InventHelp^{SM} had made for me. I picked out a pair of black pants and a long black sweater. I wanted to look nice and to be warm.

The weather report for this evening before audition day promised to be nasty. A storm was moving in, threatening six to eight inches of snow. We decided to leave around 3:30 the next morning. The trip was less than two hours under normal conditions, but the weather could prove impassible. Morning came and my dad offered to drive, but I insisted. Within our first two miles we saw eight vehicles in the ditch. They slid off the highway, and were stranded! I prayed for the owners of those cars, and also prayed that God would keep us safe. I crept along at about twenty-five miles per hour most of the way. The sky was black and in the headlights all you could see were little bits of snow everywhere. Plows could not keep the roads clear. There was about a six inch pile of snow between each lane. My dad was a stock car driver in his youth, and now he coached me with a great deal of patience. It seemed like forever, but four and half hours later, we were there.

We parked and went in to wait in line. There were about one

hundred people in front of us already. Each participant took a number and was told to prepare a pitch. I wasn't really sure what to say, but I sat down with my materials from Invent Help, opened it up and did a quick study in preparation for my sales talk. I picked out the most important points and began writing them down on a piece of paper. When I had all the information down pat, I started rehearsing to my dad. I said my lines over and over again. A small group from the show came to all of us and said, "You will have two minutes to pitch your product, and please, don't just give us statistics. We want to hear about your passion and how you believe your product will benefit the world. Just have fun and be yourself. Good luck everyone!"

After about three and half hours of waiting, it was finally my turn. After all the paperwork was turned in, we waited in another room. I practiced more and more, polishing and timing my pitch to two minutes exactly. Soon number 323 was called. I grabbed my things, including my books just in case, and tried to gather myself the best I could, making sure I was mentally prepared. I had confidence in my product, but I was going to have to sell myself as well. There were a lot of people practicing their pitches, and trying to hide their inventions as they did so. I focused all my energies inward and on my product.

"Jodi Pliszka," the voice called. I walked into center of the room, every nerve on edge. At the table was Daneil Soiseth, my judge. Daniel was one of the executive producers of the show. When I entered the room he smiled and said, "So, I hear that you are an author, too? Wow, you are talented!" I thanked him, of course, and approached the judges' table to show the two books about Bella and Gizmo. I was proud of them. Daniel looked at them quickly and made some very favorable comments.

It was time to deliver my two-minute speech. Not to boast, but I believe I can say that I nailed it. I hit all the major points and even had time to take my hair off at the end. Daniel's mouth was slightly open then it curled in a smile. "That's a great pitch, and a cool product. You can see that I am losing my hair, too, and I hope to be able to try your product out some day. Good job, Jodi, thank you!"

Dad and I had a very long but satisfying drive home. We talked about the audition the entire time. I had memorized every word of my speech and recalled it now almost word for word. My dad indulged me. He was patient and generous with his listening. Make no mistake. He was as engaged in the process as I was. The bottom line was that I did my best and there was nothing further to do, but wait to see if they would use me on TV or not.

I tried to put the show and my pitch out of my mind for a few weeks, to not obsess about it. After all, there was plenty else to do. I worked as a case management coordinator at a nearby hospital. I had a child in school. I had bought a place of our own;

a beautiful house on three-quarters of an acre with a pool. There was maintenance. There were animals.

And then, one most incredible day, I got a phone call from a lady named Davina with ABC's American Inventor. She told me I had made it to the next round of auditions and they would be sending me to LA in two weeks. I would be competing with about 300 others. She told me what to wear, where to go when I arrived and how to handle my expenses. The coming audition raised the pitch of life around us, so much so that it bordered on becoming stressful, but settled as elation.

⌘⌘⌘

A perspective. During the bustle of everyday life, we run at maximum at one time or another. How I am able to get up, work out, make breakfast, shovel snow, wake up Jess up and tend to her, shower, put clothes in the wash, make and eat breakfasts, drive Jess to school, go to the hospital, work, work, work, come home, pick up Jess, do homework, make dinner, work on writing or promoting my books, try to find a manufacturer for my Headline IT! product, play attentively with Jess, clean litter boxes, feed the animals, put the clothes in the dryer, give Jess a bath, read to her before bedtime, tuck her in, say prayers together, make lunch for the next day, pick out clothes to wear for both of us, fold the laundry, do all this before I collapse?

But then, in all the spin and frenzy of every day, some miracle happens. It happens right where it's supposed to, right in the midst of things. It strikes in the red-hot center of the inspired madness we call life. It makes sense of it all, it brings justice to the all the outrage we have ever suffered, the names we've been called or have called ourselves. Everything gets transformed by what seems to be the touch of a magic wand. For me, I somehow felt I had wandered into the world of Reality TV, or maybe some fantasy world. Then again, was all this good fortune divinely ordered? Was it part of my redemption?

Chapter Eighteen

The California Auditions

THE WEATHER WAS WARM, the people beautiful. I took a cab to the hotel, unpacked my things for the next couple days and went to work on my pitch. My call time was the next day and I was thankful for the long evening ahead.

Morning arrived quickly and was mine to do with as I pleased until the 11:00 a.m. transportation rendezvous in the hotel lobby. I'd walk, take in a few sites, practice my pitch and keep calm. Flowers were in bloom everywhere I looked: bird of paradise, agapanthus, bananas—so many beautiful exotics not found in the north. I grabbed a turkey sandwich and small soup at a deli intending to find a bench in the sun. Jess called and we chatted as I walked along. I was involved in our conversation and barely noticed what appeared to be a homeless man on the corner trying to get my attention. I kept walking and talking. When I hung up, it bothered me that I hadn't so much as acknowledged this man's existence. Homeless or famous, we all deserved at least this much. I had twenty minutes before I needed to be back to the hotel. I retraced my steps and found him. He asked me if I knew Jesus and I assured him that I did. He told me I was blessed. Softness, an inner light perhaps, something good, came through his coarse exterior. I offered him my soup and sandwich which he gladly accepted and blessed me again. We stood at the corner of Fifth and Hope. *"Blessed and hopeful indeed,"* I thought and returned to the hotel.

I was just in time. We were taken to the ABC studios in Hollywood to pitch our ideas. I nailed it again. At the end, I removed my wig and left it on the table, walking off the stage in a beam of white light with my hands raised in the air.

I went back to Wisconsin feeling confident and hopeful about the pitch. It was good, very good. But was it good enough to advance me to the Top 50?

Life had the power to amaze. I received my patent, had written and published two books, was receiving a lot of media coverage, and had gone to Los Angeles to pitch my idea.

It was difficult keeping the details of the California trip and the show to myself. My enthusiasm and expectations grew beyond my own boundaries. But the show had asked us all to sign a contract promising nondisclosure, so I was muzzled. I calmed my nerve the best I could and maintained myself adequately. I went about performing my normal duties, and yet lived with a certain expectancy concerning the next phase of the competition.

I was uncertain about how to handle things at the hospital. They needed a person in my position. I inquired about a leave of absence through Human Services and filled out the paperwork for it in advance. I would leave it in my desk drawer. If I made the next cut, my parents would contact the supervisor and have her open the envelope. I loved my job, and I wasn't completely comfortable about the prospect of a leave, but I had chosen to follow the opportunity in front of me, and in so doing, had to feel a certain agreement around me.

Davina called a few weeks later. I'd made the next cut to the Top 50 and would return to LA.

I'd be gone longer this time. I thought about how much I would miss Jess and how much she would miss me. The thought of being gone for even three days was difficult, but I'd survived one trip and I knew that I had strength to do it again. She and I both believed the sacrifice was worth the reward.

At the airport I held Jess tightly, probably too tightly. She was bigger emotionally at that moment than I was. I didn't want to let her go. There was a lot of strength within such a little girl. She said, "Mommy, you have a mission, and there are so many little kids to help, I know that I will see you soon, and be with you forever!" I started to cry. She was much better at good-bye than I was. She was cheerful, confident, and reassuring. I was proud of her. A mom is allowed that, I think. Mom and Dad were supportive, more supportive than I ever remember. Like we had all crossed some threshold together. And for the first time, my dad didn't tease me and pretend to cry when I left. I gave Jess one last kiss and then walked toward the security area. We blew each other kisses, and I disappeared inside of the airport.

⌘ ⌘ ⌘

I had packed for only a few days and ended up staying in Los Angeles for two months. I'm not at liberty to tell the particulars of what took place behind the scenes (as cool as it was), but I can share some of the basic events. I kept a diary.

The process by which contestants were dropped was incredibly stressful, for each of us involved. Being closed in a large room together, we naturally talked a lot and made friends. It was interesting seeing how other minds worked. At the same time we would experience an eerie silence or hear small, barely audible voices. Everyone was hard at work, preparing their pitch and focusing on their task at hand. Some were more concerned with their presentation than others, but everyone was serious about the competition at hand.

It was interesting sharing stories with the other inventors. And though we were all competing against each other, there was nonetheless a kind of kindred spirit that softened among us. Each time someone was eliminated it was heartbreaking not to be able to even say goodbye. They wouldn't be there for the next round and we'd probably never see them again. Emotions did strange things. Of course, you didn't want to be eliminated, and yet when someone was, you felt sad and elated at the same time. Their elimination moved you one step closer to winning and another step closer to those who remained. There were times I didn't quite know how to react. But I wasn't alone. That, too, was a common feeling, another kindred spirit among us.

It was exciting to be standing in front of the panel of judges at last. Each judge was talented and accomplished in their own given field. I grew to like them all, despite the challenge that each of them presented to me once I was before them. But I knew in my heart I had a great product. My story was strong and I knew there was an entire host of people in the world that could benefit by it. When I did my pitch, I put my heart and soul into every word. I organized the words and reorganized them for maximum effect. I told my life story (condensed, of course). I brought passion to my performance, which, once I started, seemed no longer a "pitch" but simply the expression of a product whose time had come. As the words flowed effortlessly from my mouth, I felt the presence of God giving his consent to this moment and to all the many events that brought me here. I was strong, confident, and not once was I at a loss of words. I talked about me and about my product, two things I knew better than anyone else. How could I mess up telling that?

Like the parable of the *Footprints In The Sand*, I felt that God was carrying me at that moment. After we each presented our product, we were assigned a group. They took us group by group to the judges table, one more time. We were all thrilled, but this time the pitching was over. We'd receive a verdict of yes or no. I looked around me and knew that I was in the presence of greatness. I just knew each one of us was going to progress to the next level. We walked across the studio lot in unison and into the holding room, where Liz, one of the lead producers, prepared us for the next part. We all walked on stage, and stood before Peter Jones. Peter told us that we all did a great job, and he was sorry that he had to tell us one last thing, that "We all made it to the next round!" We were down to the Top 24.

The time came for our last and final pitch. Simon Cowell came into our holding room with his entourage. He smelled of expensive cologne and cigarette smoke. He had a cigarette in one hand and a pack of cigarettes in the other. I gave him a hug. It was apparent that he worked out; he had a very firm body and a gentle touch. He kissed me on the check. I asked him to autograph one of my books for Jess. He was so gracious, so Hollywood, and called me "Jodi darling." I was in heaven and a bit star-struck as well.

Finally, Matt Gallant came in. We yelled and cheered and had a ball, giving our worn nerves a well-deserved rest. I was able to sit with him for a few moments. We fell into an easy conversation about 1 topic I thought unlikely for him. Matt had just spoken at a college about his battle with depression, a condition he had lived with his whole life. I listened as a friend and as a therapist as well. In some sense, it was reassuring to know that Matt was just a real guy, who suffered some of the same dark things the rest of us did. I offered what support I could and felt touched by the experience.

We approached the judges one at a time to do our very last pitch for this round of the competition. We were told to put our hearts and souls into this one. I am sure that's what each of us did. As I stood in front of the judges, I smiled, eager to make my presentation. I began, and in no time at all, I could see I was captivating them. The more eye contact they maintained with me, the more confidence I had. When I was done, I was exhausted. I had poured everything I had into it. Now I could allow myself to be happy, whether I made it or not.

I stood silent, waiting for the judge's verdict once again. Because this was television, the pauses were long in order to adjust camera angles and things like that. As eager as we all were, as anxious and as hopeful, we all had to practice patience. Mary Lou Quinlan was first. She was generous with her comments, very supportive of my efforts. She was a wonderful person to have at my side. She looks at products from a woman's perspective. I suspected she would see the need for Headline It! She was sensitive and intelligent, bold with her words, and a very gracious lady.

Doug Hall was challenging. I respect Doug a great deal, because he is an inventor and entrepreneur, but I know Doug never got what my idea was about. He said he couldn't see the point of wearing a diaper on you head. I was quick to reply, "Me neither." I was then able to go into the high tech wick wear material I wanted to use for my product, putting it into a whole new category. Doug agreed with me this time, and appreciated how much I had matured in my pitches. I stopped being as emotional as I had a tendency to be, and showed him the business side of my product and the huge market that could be reached.

Peter Jones was very eloquent. At first he did not see the need for my product, but as I continued to pitch it, and as he got more information about it, he seemed to change. This information allowed him to make his choice. Peter could truly see the need and the potential of my product. He told me, "You have touched the hearts of America, and clearly demonstrated that there is a need for this." I was so thrilled that Peter, one of the richest men in the world, and a successful entrepreneur, would pass such promising judgment on my product. Hearing him gave me the extra confidence I needed to push my performance into overdrive.

Ed Evangelista was the last judge, and to me, maybe the best of them all. Ed helps run one of the largest, most successful marketing agencies in New York, JWT. His instincts about products are highly evolved. He knows all about them, what will sell and what won't. From the beginning, Ed saw the need. He knew my product would sell, particularly since it was disposable. Convenience is critical these days, he would say. He argued with Peter one time, telling him that he was not going to take time to wash out the inside of a golf hat each time, when he could simply use my product and throw it away when he was done. He said time was of the essence. Anything that would make life easier for him, not only would he use, but it would carry his endorsement as well. I was honored to have him consent my product.

On the whole, the comments were very positive. I could only be hopeful that I would be picked one of the Top 12. Once again, I waited through that intolerably long pause, till Peter said, "I know that your product can help millions of people. You truly have touched the hearts of America. You are on to the next round."

I was overcome with emotion. I couldn't help myself. I was spent. I kissed Peter square on the lips as he handed me the check for fifty thousand dollars. I kissed the back of the check. I gave Mary Lou a huge kiss on the cheek and thanked her. I gave Ed kiss on the cheek and thanked him over and over again. Doug got a handshake. Sorry, Doug. As I walked off stage with the check in my hand, I said to them all, "I will make you proud. I won't let you down. You'll see!" I then raised my hands toward heaven to thank God. That seemed to be my signature footage—walking off the stage, wearing my long black sweater and disappearing into the white light with my arms in the air. Thank you, God! My dream was just about to come true!

Everyone was hugging and cheering, excited that we had actually done it! It was alright to let the guard down, to let go, to be a child for a moment or two. We had made the Top 12. It was about 12:30 in the morning and we were all punchy from the fourteen and a half hour day but we had just enough energy to celebrate with pizza and soda. I was thrilled, honored and relieved.

It was 1:00 a.m. when someone passed me their cell phone to call home. Dad answered after many rings and somewhere between my happy sobs, he heard I was on to the next round.

Chapter Nineteen

California and Coming Home

BEING AWAY FROM HOME WAS ONE THING, but having my cell phone taken away from me was another. We had no access to computers, phones, or any way to contact our families. The show wanted to protect the secrecy of the Top 12, so we were limited to calling home once a day, for about five or ten minutes. When I first found out that I couldn't talk to Jess whenever I wanted, and that I was going to miss so much of her life for the next two months, it was almost too much.

We were now sequestered in our hotel rooms and instructed to pack for a move the following morning. The new location, too, was to remain a secret. Suffice it to say, the place was amazing. It was architecturally stunning and beautifully appointed. No detail had gone unnoticed, no need was unmet. It was a complete compound where we lacked for nothing, from physical fitness to food to any kind of commissary. When I left Wisconsin, it was five degrees Fahrenheit, with a negative 20 wind chill factor. By a simple trick of geography and good fortune, I had been transported to paradise.

I hit the weights, ran five miles a day and spent whatever free time I could, rain or shine, in the Olympic sized swimming pool. The fish in me emerged and my daily swims in a bright red bandana became a trademark of sorts. I trained myself for the daily work body, mind and spirit.

My only struggle was being so isolated, cut off, from the outside world. In my room I kept my Bible in one hand and a friend's book in the other. Dan Castro's *Critical Choices That Change Lives* spoke of making hero decisions in life. Together with God's word, it gave me much needed strength and courage.

We carried beepers and were paged when it was our turn to leave the compound or do our shoot for the day. Each of us met with eighteen different companies, and had only a few minutes to interview each one. I found a suitable company for me in no time at all, T2Design. I knew that they were going to be able to help me take my product to whole new level. I chose them. And I am happy I did. We worked long hours filming and working with my company, picking out new materials for my product. We found just the right wicking materials and did all of our testing quickly. I was even allowed to help design the product packaging. I was touched to see my words and my name on every box.

Each day got easier for me. In time I was able to speak with Jess. Sometimes she cried when we talked. I did too. The separation was a trial for both of us, but at her age it had to be tougher on her. After hanging up, which was difficult enough, I went back to my room and cried. I couldn't fight back my tears. The loneliness I already felt was too overwhelming. I gave myself a good talking to and finally regained my composure. Excess emotion would not help. My future was before me. God had led me this far, and I would trust Him with the rest.

Of course, I prayed for both of us. Praying had become a habit, a good one. With all the energy and movement around me, with all the distance and the unknowns a mother can feel for her absent child, I found myself appealing to God more and more, just to keep up, to keep my emotions and my ambitions in line with each other. Nothing on this earth is more important than my child's well being. Mom was great with Jess. She softened much of my grief.

One day we got a big surprise. We were being flown back home the next day to be filmed with our families. We were to show and tell more about how we developed our ideas. Even though we'd be back in twenty-four hours, I was thrilled.

I was home! Jess slept with me that night, and I prayed all night long. I spent hours watching her sleep and stroking her face from time to time, enjoying the tender closeness of her. I wanted to memorize the night and every detail of her face, I'd need them

160

in two thousand miles. After three weeks apart, I appreciated this little girl more than ever and cherished our relationship—one in which there was so much gentleness and respect.

I was still awake and practically making myself sick with the grief of leaving her. I wasn't new to separation anxiety. As a little girl I had an abnormal fear that my parents wouldn't return if they went out for an evening. My dad teased me with mock tears about my crying and clinging to them. Instead of shaming me, his attempts to reduce my anxiety added fierceness to it. Now I prayed that God would give me strength to handle this like an adult. Near morning, I fell asleep at last.

I dreamed about the old man on the sidewalk at Fifth Street and Hope. I had been thinking about my next pitch and what I was going to do to make an even greater impact this time. Then, it came to me. Hope. That's it. I would pitch my idea to start a foundation called HOPE that would give back proceeds from the HEADLINE IT! to those in need. I worked my dream into an acronym. H would represent the headliner. O, oil. P, perspiration. And E, elimination. HOPE.

All the men and women in the armed forces need HOPE. They need the real thing, and they need my product which will go by the same name. Cancer patients and alopecia sufferers all need HOPE. My little man standing at Fifth and Hope gave me the idea of a lifetime. I knew that this would add a new measure of perfect to my pitch.

The filming went fine and fast and I was leaving again. Parting with my family was worse than it had been before— I'd be away for five weeks this time. I felt more like I was going to prison than the airport, but the tearful goodbye ended and I was off again.

The next few weeks were very busy. There was consolation in the distraction. I made friends with Sharon, the bathroom survival kit person, and Sheryl, the Inbrella lady, but my most fortunate friendship was Bobby the Toner Belt guy. Bobby and I had a lot in common, and talked easily, and forever. Ironically, we were competing against each other for the next spot. Yet it never seemed to matter to either of us. We shared the same philosophies about life. He liked swimming with me, to think and relax. Bobby is a great guy.

I lived a few doors down from Joe and Jenny Safuto, the Pureflush people. Jen was as kind as she was lovely, and Joe was like a brother to me. He loved to tease me about being bald, making comments about my shining bald head scaring little kids. Whenever I was really sad, I could go to their room, and Joe always made me smile. They became my best friends.

One Friday we were told it would be the last time we would be able to speak with our families for a while. This made me angry. Jess had already lost four teeth while I was gone, and this weekend the finals were to be held in Madison for the Odyssey of the Mind competition, which she was a part of. I was the coach, and left it to my dearest friend Pam Schulties to pick up the pieces when I left.

And of course, Mom. But rules were rules, and we had to follow them. For the next week I was not able to speak with my family.

We all worked hard to complete a year's worth of work in eight weeks, and we all succeeded. It was now time to go up against the judges and do our final pitch. We were all put into a holding room, again, where we wished each other the best of luck. Most of us were quite content with how far our products had come.

We weren't supposed to speak with the other people on the other teams, but we did manage a few "good lucks" to each other on the way to and from the bathroom. It was a very long day. I didn't finish my last pitch until after 11:00 p. m. Filming was complete sometime after midnight and we then had to wait to face the judges for the deliberation. I was thrilled with my pitch. To watch Doug Hall do a turn-around was reward in itself. At first he told me he couldn't see how my product was going to work. Then, after further scrutiny, he became a believer. That was great. MaryLou questioned me about the cost of the product, and I was able to show her how we arrived at our numbers. She was satisfied, as all the judges were, and there were no negative comments said to me concerning my last pitch. Peter felt that I had utilized my $50,000 exceptionally well, and thought that I had come further then any other contestant with my product. He told me how proud he was of me, and again, how I touched the hearts of America. I was thrilled and tired, all in one.

Ed thought that I had proved my point and said "she answered all the questions that I had and more. She clearly demonstrated the market and the need for the product. I think that people will buy her product." He was pleased with my performance and my product testing results. The firemen loved my product, and it actually stopped the sweat from rolling into their eyes and prevented their goggles from becoming fogged. The ladies that had cancer and alopecia that tried the product loved it, as well. I knew that whatever happened, I was thrilled to have been able to take my product all the way in this program. I was ready for manufacturing.

I wanted to see Jess badly. Her birthday was only a few days away, and I didn't want to miss her turning ten! When Peter told me that I was going home, I was ecstatic. I smiled and thanked him profusely. I was going to see my baby soon. I cried as I left the stage, because I was finally able to go home. We went back to the hotel at about 2:00 a. m. and I was told that I had to have all of my things packed and be in the lobby three hours later. After seventeen hours of shooting, I had to pack and be ready to go. The excitement of seeing Jess was stronger than my tiredness.

I was taken to the airport, along with a producer. They were following me, to film my big home coming. They still wouldn't let me have my cell phone. As excited as I was to see my baby, I was told that I wouldn't see her until the next morning. I wasn't held against my will or anything, but they begged me to not see her yet. They wanted the genuine reaction of my family members. I conceded. They weren't necessarily overt about it, but nonetheless, they seemed to threaten me a bit, saying that they "might not edit me in a good light." I followed the rules and was so exhausted, I passed out. I woke early the next morning with one thing on my mind. I was like a child. The limo picked me up at the hotel and the camera crew followed. They went to my parents' home, where Jess was, and filmed my family awaiting my arrival. I had to sit in the limo a few blocks away for one hour, waiting.

The limo driver finally said, "Okay, it's time." I jumped in the car, of course. The cameraman was sitting in the front seat, filming me. Tears began streaming down my cheek, as my producer asked me questions about coming home. I said "I am ready to resume my place as Mommy!" We approached my parents' driveway, and I could see the *Welcome Home Mommy* banner on the house. I thought I would jump out of the car at that moment. It was like Christmas, Birthday, and the day I gave birth to Jessica all rolled into one.

They stopped the limo and I was given direction to wait until the door opened and I saw Jess, before I left the car. The moment I saw my beautiful little girl I threw open the door, threw my briefcase to the ground, and ran to her with all my might. Jess ran towards me as well. The slap of our bodies making contact was audible, we hugged long and hard. Jess had a rose in her hand for me, and tears streaming down her cheeks. I was crying so hard and hugging her so hard, and the feel of her soft cheeks on my lips was like the touch of heaven. I was finally home! The cameras were right in our faces, and neither of us seemed to even notice. They had to do their jobs I suppose. Still, this was a new best day of my life.

I hugged my dad with one arm, while holding Jess, and then my mom. They both were relieved I had come back home, and could take up my life again. They commented that I had never looked better. I was tan and fit, wearing new clothes and the pricey wig the show bought for me. All this and a fresh application of permanent cosmetic makeup helped me feel refreshed and ready to begin the next phase of my life.

Something in this moment brought Grandma to mind. I sensed her watching me like a guardian angel, guiding me as she always had. She'd never let me forget that love and memories last forever.

At last we went in the house. Jess sat on my lap and began to show me the four holes in her mouth where teeth had been. I couldn't stop smiling and kissing her. She was holding my hand, we were together again, and we were never letting go of each other.

They even interviewed Jess. "I am so glad that my mommy is back. I missed her more than anything. Even though she didn't win the big prize, my mommy is worth more than a million dollars to me!" I cried, of course, and that made for a great wrap up for the camera crew. We said our goodbyes to the film crew and my producer. I got my cell phone back! Having no cell phone helped me learn that I don't really need to be at everyone's disposal when they call. Cell phone or no cell phone, nothing mattered. I was home. I was in my world again.

Chapter Twenty

20/20

I got back on April 7th, in time for Jess' birthday on the 9th! To be reunited with her and our animals in our own home was marvelous. I had missed our pets: Gizmo, Bella, Grace, and Cuddles, our bunny, and I could tell they had missed me too. In their purrs and snuggles and wriggles was almost more unconditional love one could hold. Almost.

Jess would be ten years old. She had always wanted a puppy, so on her birthday we went to see Kristen. She had become a dear friend since we first found Bella. Now, she gave us a white Chihuahua pup. It was only eight weeks old. He was a perfect fit for Jess. Kristen also had two chocolate Sphynx brothers that needed a home. Did we want them—what do you think? Our family doubled in the blinking of an eye. We named the Chihuahua Chico and the Sphynx cats Riggley and Ripley. The birthday seemed to last more than just one day. The celebration went on and on. We were all happy to be together again. Our spirits were light.

Now that I was home and the show was airing, I was still not allowed to tell anyone who made it into the top four on the show. I did about six television interviews, two magazines, five newspapers, and even had my own commercial on TV. I couldn't help but feel the celebrity effect of the show, but I think I stayed fairly grounded. There was a lot going on around me and inside me. After all the time and effort I put into the show, I was actually a bit tired of being on camera. But I focused on my product more now and getting it to market. I took Jess with me to every interview. A few times she was on television with me. I wanted to include her as much as I could.

I met a wonderful man named Scott Lazerson, who is a PR agent and an amazing networking talent. I hired him to help me keep the momentum of the show rolling. I threw out the first pitch at a Brewers game, with Jess next to me on the mound. I met the Admirals hockey team, got a puck for Jess, and stayed and watched the game, as a guest star. I rode with Jess in the Fourth of July Parade. We were becoming more and more visible.

I lost my job at the hospital while on the show, and needed income, quickly. I had worked with InventHelp[SM] prior to going on the show. They had prepared the statistics book that helped me make it on the show. I'd call the owners of the company and tell them my story. Maybe they would want to hire me in some capacity. They were a big part of the success I had achieved. I spoke with Martin Berger, the owner of Techno Systems and InventHelp[SM].

He welcomed me as part of the team. I signed a year's contract with InventHelp^{SM} as spokesperson and flew out to the INPEX convention to meet with Martin and many of the other employees. They treated me royally. INPEX is an invention trade show, the largest of its kind in the country. Most of the inventors had watched the show and knew who I was. There were autographs all around. I met up with Joe, the Pureflush Top 12 friend, and Erik and Francisco, who were in the top four from the show. They were there to speak and meet with the inventors and it was great to see them again. It was like a reunion, especially now that we could be friends and not competitors.

I called Jess as often as I could. Sometimes we spoke every hour, just because we could. I was only gone for four days this time, and Jess was totally cool with that. She knew that I was now working my new job as spokesperson for the company, and she could call me whenever she wanted to.

The show finally ended and it was time to come home. As I stepped off the plane, I found myself jogging to the gates. I couldn't wait to see Jess again. My heart was racing. And there she was. I threw down my bags and hugged her, twirling in a circle together and laughing. This is what happiness looks like, and feels like, and probably sounds like. All laughs and small talk.

My life had changed. I had been seen by over 20 million people, and I was going to do whatever I could to keep my bald head in the news! Next, I would promote Headline It! I would have a waiting period until Freemantle released us from our contracts. Finally, in July, the letter came releasing me from their options. We were ready to go at last. I assembled a team to prepare our business plan and began working on setting up the foundation of the company. I was e-mailing back and forth with Ed Evangelista, the New York judge from the show. He was willing to help with Headline It! and work with my team.

In the back of my mind, I always felt badly that I had promised Jess she could come to California. I wanted her to view it as a good place rather than the state that took her mommy away for two months. So when the opportunity arose in August to do radio and television commercials in California for InventHelp℠ I bought Jess a ticket. I wasn't leaving without her this time. We cut loose and had the time of our lives. Touring Hollywood, spending four days at Disneyland experiencing it through her eyes, and swimming in the Pacific was a dream come true for both of us. I couldn't remember ever having so much fun.

As soon as we returned home, I began submitting HEADLINE IT! to manufacturers until I found just the right fit, Jast Company. After months of working through the details of packaging and material selection, we are finally ready to begin manufacturing. Another dream has become reality.

Looking back, as you do when so much history has passed, perhaps losing my hair wasn't the horror I once felt it to be. "Hindsight is 20/20," they all say. I lived with hair for twenty years. I lived without hair for twenty more. And I am happy with distances I've come in my forty years. I only pray that the next forty will be just as exciting. But that reminds me, I have one last debt of gratitude to pay. No doubt, the greatest debt of all, and that is to God. He got me here. I know that. Not on my strength, but His. And I'm grateful. Not only that, but I feel His pleasure in just being me. The creature giving back to the Creator what is rightly His. After all, He knows the number of hairs on our heads. It's just that some of us are less work than others. God bless you all!

"There is no greater gift than knowing our purpose in life."
—Jodi Pliszka, M.S.

Jodi Pliszka, M.S. a TOP 12 FINALIST on ABC TV'S American Inventor Reality TV show. Jodi is the inventor of the Award Winning, Revolutionary "HEADLINE IT!" product, an award winning author, motivational speaker, business owner and proud Mommy. Jodi presently resides in Wisconsin with her daughter Jessica, and their hairless kitties, and family close by.

Go to www.headlineit.net for more information.

"Bella and Gizmo's Adventures : The Hairless Sphnyx Cats" and "Bella Get's A New Sweater" are two charming and engaging children's books that deal with the personal and difficult subject of hair loss. The main characters are Sphynx cats, which is a breed of hairless cat. These cuddly characters realize that their differences are strengths in disguise, that they are loveable just as they are, and they go through the struggle of loneliness, finding friendship and love, as well as companionship in each other's hairlessness.

To purchse all of Jodi's books, and the Bella Doll
go to www.jodipliszka.npauthors.com
and to www.nightengalepress.com

Jodi's books are the recipient of the
Adding Wisdom Award
from <u>www.parenttoparent.com</u>

LaVergne, TN USA
26 January 2011
214042LV00003B/46/A